ALBANIA *and the* ALBANIANS
in the ANNUAL REPORTS *of the*
AMERICAN BOARD *of* COMMISSIONERS
for FOREIGN MISSIONS, 1820–1924

ALBANIA *and the* ALBANIANS
in the ANNUAL REPORTS *of the*
AMERICAN BOARD OF COMMISSIONERS
for FOREIGN MISSIONS,
1820–1924

COMPILED AND EDITED
by DAVID HOSAFLOOK

Part of the 500/200
Albanian Protestant Commemorative Series
General Editor, David Hosaflook

Albania and the Albanians in the Annual Reports of the American Board of Commissioners for Foreign Missions, 1820–1924

Published by the Institute for Albanian and Protestant Studies with the permission of Wider Church Ministries of the United Church of Christ (formerly the American Board of Commissioners for Foreign Missions).

This version © David Hosaflook, 2017.

All rights reserved. No part of this publication may be reproduced in any form or by any electronic or mechanical means, including information storage and retrieval systems, without written permission from the publisher, except in the case of brief quotations embodied in critical reviews and certain other noncommercial uses permitted by copyright law.

ISBN 978-1-946244-07-9

Publisher's Cataloging-in-Publication data

Names: Hosaflook, David, compiler and editor.

Title: Albania and the Albanians in the annual reports of the American Board of Commissioners for Foreign Missions, 1820-1924 / compiled and edited by David Hosaflook.

Series: The 500/200 Albanian Protestant Commemorative Series

Description: Includes index. | Tirana, Albania: Institute for Albanian and Protestant Studies, 2017.

Identifiers: ISBN 978-1-946244-06-2 (Albania printing) | 978-1-946244-07-9 (pbk.) | 978-1-946244-08-6 (ebook)

Subjects: LCSH American Board of Commissioners for Foreign Missions–History–19th century. | American Board of Commissioners for Foreign Missions–History–20th century. | Missions–Albania. | Balkan Peninsula–History–19th century--Sources. | Balkan Peninsula–History--20th century–Sources. | Albania--History–1820-1924–Sources.

Classification: LCC DR43 .H67 2017 | DDC 949.602/8–dc23

www.instituti.org

to Dr. Arben and Linda Bushgjokaj

Introduction

THE AMERICAN BOARD OF COMMISSIONERS FOR Foreign Missions (ABCFM) was America's first great Protestant missionary society and played a significant role in establishing the Albanian Evangelical Protestant Movement in the late 1800s, a movement with both a religious and educational emphasis. This resource is a compilation of portions from the ABCFM's annual reports concerning its work with Albanians. The American missionaries' efforts unfolded in the context of great political and social changes in the Ottoman Empire and the Balkans; therefore, this work also contains information about other nations insofar as such information assists readers to understand the evolution of missionary work among the Albanians.

The ABCFM was established in 1810, inspired by the missionary zeal of American college students. Four years previously, Samuel Mills and other students from Williams College in Williamstown, Massachusetts, began praying together regularly in the open air. One August evening, a thunderstorm sent them scurrying to find shelter under a haystack, where they prayed specifically for the evangelization of the world. The gathering became known as the "Haystack Prayer Meeting," and the location became memorialized as the birthplace of American foreign missions.¹ Under the haystack the students determined "to send the saving Gospel of Jesus Christ to non-Christians in a foreign land" and established a prayer society for this purpose.²

Artist rendering of the Haystack Prayer Meeting (© Frank Soltesz) and photo of the Haystack Monument at Williams College (public domain). The monument bears the inscription, "The Field is the World. The Birthplace of American Foreign Missions, 1806. Samuel J. Mills, James Richards, Francis L. Robbins, Harvey Loomis, Byram Green".

---

1 *Proceedings of the Ninety-Seventh Annual Meeting of the American Board of Commissioners for Foreign Missions.* Boston: ABCFM, 1907, 4.

2 Putney, Clifford. *The Role of the American Board in the World: Bicentennial Reflections on the Organization's Missionary Work, 1810–2010.* Edited by Clifford Putney and Paul T. Burlin. Eugene, Oregon: Wipf & Stock, 2012, 1.

Four years later, while completing their theological training at Andover Theological Seminary, Mills and four friends (Adoniram Judson, Gordon Hall, Samuel Newell, and Samuel Nott) presented their vision to their faculty and a group of church leaders, expressing their desire to become missionaries and seeking prayer and counsel. They also asked whether they should attempt to join European missionary societies or expect the American churches to create their own society.[3] The church leaders affirmed the students' desire, and by September of 1810 the ABCFM was established.[4]

The mission of the Board was singular and clear, as expressed in its second annual report:

> The cause is God's, and it must succeed. The object is the salvation of men; the furtherance of the great purpose for which the Redeemer came down from heaven and died—the extension of his kingdom and the advancement of his glory. In this cause, therefore, we have every Christian inducement to "be steadfast and immovable, always abounding in the work of the Lord, for as much as we know, that our labor will not be in vain in the Lord."[5]

---

3 *The First Ten Reports of the American Board of Commissioners for Foreign Missions with other documents of the board*. Boston: ABCFM, 1836, "Minutes of the First Annual Meeting," 9–10.

4 Dwight, Henry Otis, H. Allen Tupper, Jr., and Edwin M. Bliss. *The Encyclopedia of Missions: Descriptive, Historical, Biographical, Statistical*. New York: Funk & Wagnalls, 1904, 26–27.

5 *The First Ten Reports*, "Minutes of the Second Annual Meeting," 15-24. Quote from the New Testament, 1 Corinthians 15:58.

The ABCFM commissioned their first five missionaries on February 7, 1812, with instructions that would be repeated to missionaries in subsequent years. They were first to maintain personal purity and fervor by regular Bible reading and prayer. They were to pursue love with one another and to avoid conflicts among themselves. They were to cooperate with other Protestant missionary groups. They were to be culturally sensitive, causing no offenses as guests in their new countries. They were to remember that their primary purpose was to give "the saving knowledge of Christ." They were to avoid politics. And they were to learn the language of the people as a "matter of primary attention."[6]

The first missionaries of the ABCFM to the Ottoman Empire—Levi Parsons and Pliny Fisk—arrived in Smyrna (today's Izmir, Turkey) in 1820 in a mission to the Jews. Two years later, the ABCFM installed a printing press in Malta to supply the Mediterranean with Christian books and brochures.

As missionaries established their presence in a particular location and began working with a particular nationality, they simultaneously set their sights on new locations and learned about peoples still uninformed about the Gospel. They continually made tours to regions beyond their current locations and issued appeals for more funding and more laborers. Their role model was the Apostle Paul, who had heard a "Macedonian call" (cf. New Testament,

---

6 Ibid., "Minutes of the Third Annual Meeting," 38–42.

Acts 16:9-10) and who continually moved on to new areas—such as Illyricum—where the Gospel was not yet being preached (Romans 15:19-20). With such a mindset, it was only a matter of time before the ABCFM would discover the Albanian people, begin writing about them, and develop strategies to evangelize them.

As early as 1832, the distinguished ABCFM missionary and linguist Elias Riggs mentioned the Albanian language and in 1847 he mentioned the Albanians. He lamented that Albanian Christians did not have their own liturgical language and were attending church services in ancient Greek. "This very circumstance," said Riggs, "has tended to rouse a feeling of nationality, and a desire to cultivate their own language. The nation feels the want of a language for the expression of religious ideas, of which they can comprehend at least something."[7]

The ABCFM was not, however, the first evangelical agency to become involved with the Albanian people. The British and Foreign Bible Society had been interested in the Albanians since 1816, translating and publishing Matthew's Gospel in 1824. It was the first full book of the Bible ever to be printed in Albanian. Three years later the entire Albanian New Testament was published.

Although these two volumes were a triumph for the Albanian language and people, there was a fundamental problem: most Albanians could not read. Of the few who could, most were only trained to read foreign languages

---

7 "Proceedings of the American Oriental Society." *Journal of the American Oriental Society* 1, no. 4 (1849): xxv–lxxiii, lvii–lviii.

such as Greek, Latin, Arabic, or Ottoman Turkish. There was no recognized Albanian alphabet, despite sporadic attempts by religious priests and the forward-thinking Albanian patriot, Naum Veqilharxhi. For this reason the 1827 Albanian New Testament was prepared in a modified Greek alphabet—a solution that was pragmatic for the times but became problematic later when Albanians sought to unite behind one alphabet and repudiate the notion that Orthodox Albanians should be considered Greek.

If the Albanians were ever to read the Bible in their mother tongue and if they were ever to unite as a nation, it was clear that they would need Albanian grammars and schools. The British and Foreign Bible Society was not permitted or equipped to establish schools or colleges, but the ABCFM was—and did.

Initially the ABCFM's interest in the Albanian people developed indirectly, under the auspices of its mission stations nearest to Albanian-populated territories, for example the Mission to Greece and the Western Turkey Mission. Later the European Turkey Mission and the Balkan Mission (see map on next page) were formed, bringing the Albanians directly into their purview. In 1859 Cyrus Hamlin (founder of Robert College in Istanbul) toured Macedonia and reported the existence of Albanians and the suitability of Monastir as a new mission station. Fourteen years later this recommendation was finally realized, as the ABCFM sent American missionary families to Monastir and made contact with young Gerasim Kyrias. The missionaries mentored Kyrias and educated him in

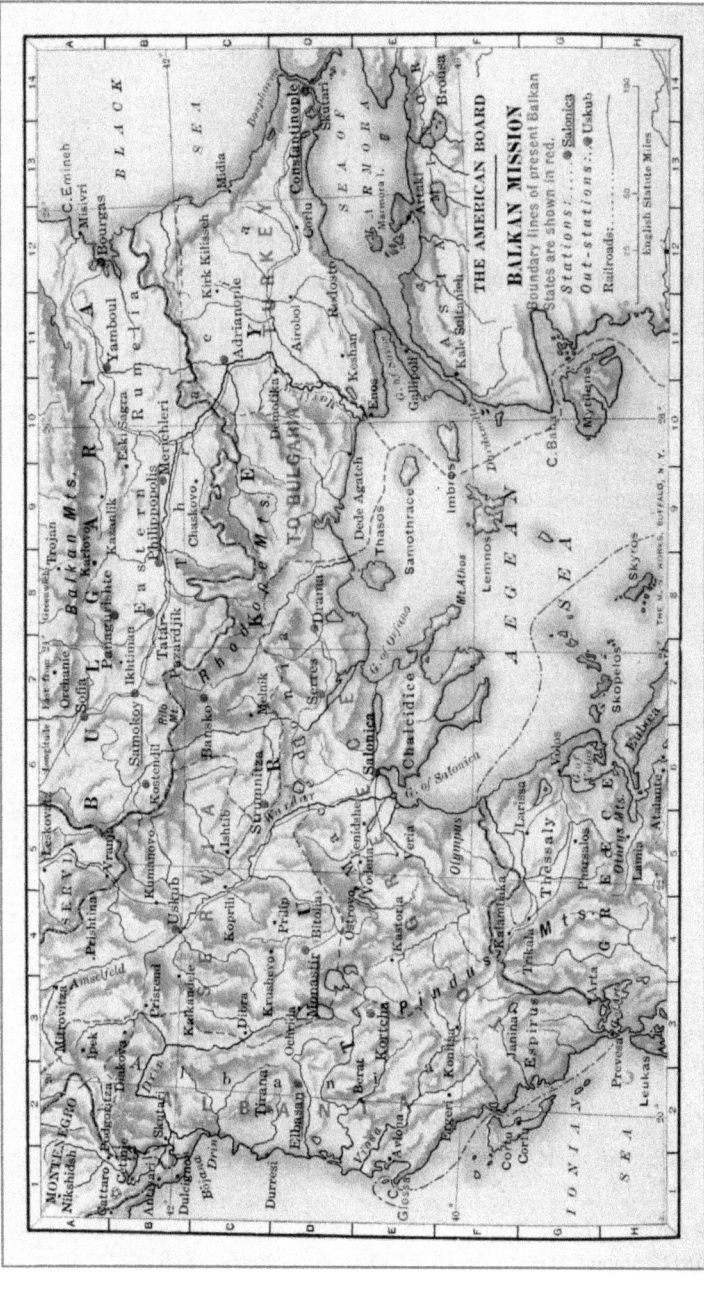

their schools in Monastir and Samokov, Bulgaria. The ABCFM also educated his brother George in Samokov and his sisters Sevasti and Paraskevi in Constantinople.

The Kyrias siblings were not only pioneers of the early Albanian Protestant movement but also pioneers of Albanian education, especially female education. In 1890 Gerasim was ordained in Monastir as Albania's first Protestant preacher. In 1891 Gerasim and Sevasti went to Kortcha and founded one of the first Albanian schools for girls. That same year Gerasim founded the first Albanian Evangelical Church. A year later an Evangelical Brotherhood was formed, "having as its sole object the development of the Albanian language and the extension of the knowledge of the Gospel."[8]

The school and the evangelical work in Korça (Kortcha) awakened strong opposition from political and religious authorities. American Protestant missionaries interceded for and assisted the work from their bases in Monastir and Istanbul, but the ABCFM did not send American missionary families—Phineas and Violet Kennedy, and Charles and Carrie Erickson—to live permanently in Korça until 1908. An American presence protected both the church and school from attempts by political and religious forces to close them down, especially during the city's most dangerous times. The Ericksons moved on to work in Tirana and Elbasan. In 1919 they retired from the ABCFM and continued working independently

---

8 Kyrias, Gerasim. "Fraternal Epistle written at Kortcha, Year I – November, 1892". Shipley to Blunt, March 25, 1893, Public Records Office, FO 78.

in Albania from 1921 to 1934, founding the Agricultural School in Kavaya. The Kennedys remained in Korça until 1921 when the ABCFM was forced to abandon their work in Albania for lack of funds. The Kennedys continued to work in Korça until 1933 under the auspices of the Albanian Evangelical Mission.

Protestant missionaries wrote copiously about Albanian territories and their experiences with the Albanian people. Their reports and letters make up an enormous body of writings about Albania that rivals the writings of foreign diplomats and travelers such as Johann Georg von Hahn and Edith Durham. There is a difference in genre, however. Whereas the travel writings focus on ethnographical and linguistic research, the missionary writings focus on the progress of their literary, evangelistic and educational work. This is not to say that the missionary writings do not provide ethnographical observations. On the contrary, they contain important insights into the social, religious, political and economic circumstances of the times, not merely as those traveling through Albania and meeting Albanians but as those who were trying to live and work among them long term.

During the times of Albanian communism, when the authorities painted a black and white world in which anything Western or religious was bad, Albanian historians had limited access to the archives of Protestant missionary societies. Figures like Gerasim Kyrias and Sevasti Kyrias presented a problem for the communists. On the one hand they were clearly Albanian patriots whose pioneering efforts in education played a significant role in Albania's national awareness and its very existence as a political nation. On the other hand, they had worked with a British Bible society and an American Protestant missionary society. Therefore, an alternative narrative was pushed: the Kyrias siblings were not really believers but had merely—and brilliantly—used the religious societies for their patriotic aims. The revisionism was convenient, winsome and logical; and without access to primary source material (most of which was located in archives outside of Albania), this narrative could neither be confirmed or denied.

Each year the ABCFM held an annual meeting at a prominent city in America to discuss their progress all over the world. After the meeting they printed a detailed annual report with selected information. The Albanians are first mentioned in these reports, in passing, in 1827. Again they are mentioned in 1852 and again in 1859. From 1872–1924 they are mentioned in nearly every successive report.

The information in the annual reports was intended to be a condensed summary of the ABCFM's missionary work as reported by its missionaries. In this volume I have combined all the Albanian-specific information from all the reports with the purpose of providing a broad overview of the scope and flow of the board's progress. Hence, it is like looking at a rainforest from the eye of a drone, not like analyzing the forest's leaves through the lens of a microscope. The Institute for Albanian and Protestant Studies (IAPS) has decided to publish this overview first,

Participants in an Annual Meeting of the ABCFM in the USA, early 1900s. Courtesy of the Library of Congress.

before publishing the missionaries' correspondence, not only because it is easier but also because it provides the context necessary for understanding the more specific narratives and events.

These pages do not focus exclusively on Albania but also on the Ottoman Empire, Bulgaria, Macedonia and Greece in order to provide context. The Albanian missionary outstation in 1891 was a part of the Monastir station founded in 1873, which grew out of the Samokov station founded in 1869, which grew out of the Eski Zagra station founded in 1859, and so on. The strategies and models of evangelism and establishing girls schools were copied and adapted in each station. Hence, the development of the work in Albania must be analyzed in the greater context of a cohesive missionary strategy unfolding in the Ottoman Empire and the Balkans. With this in mind, we have tried to provide as much information as necessary for readers and historians to connect the dots.

This resource is being published together with a companion volume of the same nature: *Albania and the Albanians in the Annual Reports of the British and Foreign Bible Society, 1805–1955*. The ABCFM and the BFBS must be studied together to understand the cooperation of both societies, the evolution of the Albanian Protestant Movement, and the impact this movement made on the Albanian national cause. Both volumes coincide with the worldwide commemoration of the 500th anniversary of the Protestant Reformation and are part of a jubilee year for Albanian Protestants in Albania, Kosovo, and Macedonia.

Other works related to the Albanian Protestant Movement have also been published as part of this series such as Sevasti Kyrias Dako's autobiography, Gerasim Kyrias's account of his captivity as a hostage, John Quanrud's biography of Gerasim Kyrias, and this writer's Ph.D. dissertation, *The Protestant Movement among the Albanians, 1816–1908*.

This book is also available in Albanian, translated by my friend and academic mentor, Professor Xhevat Lloshi. It is our hope that these and other writings will highlight a little known segment of Albanian history and inspire Albanians to engage in further studies on this fascinating and neglected branch of Albanian historiography.

David Hosaflook
Tirana, 2017

REPORT

OF THE

AMERICAN BOARD OF COMMISSIONERS

FOR

FOREIGN MISSIONS,

PRESENTED AT THE

FORTY-EIGHTH ANNUAL MEETING,

HELD IN

PROVIDENCE, RHODE ISLAND,

September 8—11, 1857.

BOSTON:
PRESS OF T. R. MARVIN & SON, 42 CONGRESS STREET.
1857.

Title page of one of the ABCFM Annual Reports

1810

Report from the 1st Annual Meeting
Farmington, Connecticut
September 5, 1810

Page 11
Excerpts from the original Constitution:
1. The Board shall be known by the name and style of the American Board of Commissioners for Foreign Missions.
2. The object of this Board is to devise, adopt, and prosecute, ways and means for propagating the gospel among those who are destitute of the knowledge of Christianity.

1811–1819

Reports from the 2nd–10th Annual Meetings
No pertinent information

1820

Report from the 11th Annual Meeting
The House of Henry Hudson, Esq., Hartford, Connecticut
September 20–21, 1820

Pages 32–33
At Smyrna [Levi Parsons and Pliny Fisk] found the most satisfactory evidence, that the shores of the Mediterranean

present many extensive fields of missionary labor. ... There are many professed Christians, to whom immediate access can be gained, and who would receive religious books with gladness. Christian missionaries may reside in any part of Turkey, so far as appears, without the least apprehension of interference from the government.

Rev. Mr. Williamson to the ABCFM secretary, from Smyrna, February, 1820 (*extracts*):
"Within the last fifty years, literature is beginning to peep out among the Greeks from her hiding places in Turkey. Some of the best informed are acquainted with the history of the Reformation; and will grant that Luther was a great man, sent for the benefit of the human race, though they are far at present from desiring a like reformation. Luther and those other reformers, who did not condemn and sweep away episcopal superintendence, are respected by a few of the Greeks, though the majority will have nothing to do with reformation, and know nothing about it. Besides the Christians all around the shores of the Mediterranean, those of Egypt, Abyssinia, Arabia, Syria, Persia, Asia Minor, Russia, and Turkey in Europe, of whatever denomination they may be, all have their own episcopal magistrates in ecclesiastical affairs; and each party has fixed laws for clergy and laity, of which the violation of the most trifling these ignorant people consider as more heinous, than of the most important law of the state."

1821

Report from the 12th Annual Meeting
No pertinent information

1822

Report from the 13th Annual Meeting
The Philosophical Chamber of Yale College,
New Haven, Connecticut
September 12–13, 1822

Page 75

As more is learned respecting countries on the borders of the Mediterranean, the importance of this vast field of labor is more clearly seen: and though the progress of good designs may here be uncommonly slow at first, there is no reason to doubt that their ultimate success will be peculiarly great and joyful.

1823

Report from the 14th Annual Meeting
The Court House, Boston, Massachusetts
September 17–18, 1823

Page 125

Field for missionary enterprise — In regard to the demand for evangelical laborers, the missionaries express themselves thus: "It is our united opinion, that an addition of laborers is extremely desirable in the extensive regions that border on the Mediterranean ..."

It must be obvious to every intelligent and reflecting man, that the countries around the Mediterranean furnish one of the largest, most interesting, and most inviting fields of missionary labor, which the world now presents.

1824

Report from the 15th Annual Meeting
The State House, Hartford, Connecticut
September 15–17, 1824

Page 111
The tracts printed at Malta, have been sent into Egypt, Syria, the Morea, and the Ionian Islands, and the information which has been received from different quarters has contributed to strengthen the hopes of the Committee, as to the great and permanent utility of the printing establishment. ... There can be no doubt but the demand for tracts and for larger works, in the languages prevalent around the Mediterranean, will fully equal all the probable issues from as many missionary presses, as can be put in operation.

1825

Report from the 16th Annual Meeting
No pertinent information

1826

Report from the 17th Annual Meeting
Middletown, Connecticut
September 14–15, 1826

Page 98

In June last, three more young men, descendants of the ancient Greeks, arrived in Boston, for the purpose of obtaining an education under the care of this Board. The name of the first is Gregory Perdicari. He is a native of Berea, about 22 years of age. ...He is of a respectable family, which has been reduced to poverty by Turkish oppression;—takes the Bible as his guide, and renounces the superstitions of the Greek church; is a good scholar in ancient Greek, and speaks Italian, Turkish, and Illyriac.

1827

Report from the 18th Annual Meeting
Presbyterian Church on Pearl Street, New York
October 10–15, 1827

Page 40

As the mission heretofore denominated Palestine, on account of its being specially designed for the Holy Land, is in fact brought to bear upon other countries in that region, it is thought proper to adopt a more general appellation, and to call it the mission for Western Asia. It might indeed, with still greater propriety, be called a mission to countries bordering on the Mediterranean, and to the Islands of that Sea; but so long a name would be quite inconvenient. The greater part of the evangelical operations, connected with this mission, will probably be directed to the continent of Asia, though it is hoped that Europe and Africa will continue to have some share in them.

Pages 48–49
Greek invasion [of Beirut] — On the 19th of March, 1826, the missionaries were in great danger, in consequence of a Greek squadron arriving, and attacking the city. Twelve armed vessels anchored in the river, and landed 500 men. An unsuccessful attack was made, the Turks being able to repel their assailants from the walls. Some lives were lost; and the Greeks encamped for several days in the neighborhood. They traversed the suburbs, entering houses, eating, drinking, and in some instances, pillaging. Mr. [William] Goodell's house, which stood without the walls in quite an exposed situation, was visited by many parties of them; but, on learning that he was under English protection, they quietly went away, some of them receiving religious tracts in their own language. The Emir Beshir arrived from the mountains with his troops on the 22d, and the Pasha of Acre, with his Bedouins and Albanians on the 23d. At the approach of the latter the Greeks retired, having accomplished nothing but to fill the country with violence and confusion, and to bring down upon their brethren, of the Greek population, the most cruel persecutions and sufferings. The day on which the

Pasha's troops arrived, they dispersed themselves, in small parties, for the sake of plunder.

1828

Report from the 19th Annual Meeting
First Presbyterian Church, Philadelphia
October 1–3, 1828

Page 35
The countries around the Mediterranean are, from year to year, regarded with deeper interest.

1829

Report from the 20th Annual Meeting
First Presbyterian Church, Albany, New York
October 7–9, 1829

Page 36
The countries around the Mediterranean, and accessible from its shores, will ultimately present most important and promising fields of missionary labor. Some delay must be experienced from the war, in which the Turkish empire is now engaged; and there may be temporary disappointments from other causes. But there can be no doubt that Protestant Christendom should stand ready to enter at every proper avenue, and to engage, so far as may be practicable, in every kind of evangelical exertion.

Page 43

Mr. [Rufus] Anderson arrived at Malta on the first of January [and] came to conclusions, so far as was then practicable, as to the best manner of disposing of the resources within our reach, for the benefit of the people around the Mediterranean;—left Malta for the Ionian islands, about the last of February;—visited Corfu, Ithaca, Cephalonia and Zante, in company with Mr. Smith, (who left the American mission press to the charge of Mr. Goodell), and with Mr. Robertson, the missionary from the Episcopal church in the United States;—had the pleasure of meeting Professor Bambas at Corfu, and Mr. Lowndes, of the London Missionary Society;—made the necessary inquiries, in regard to the state of things at these islands;—and left them for the Morea, about the middle of April.

1830

Report from the 21st Annual Meeting
At Old South Church, Boston
October 6–9, 1830

Page 50

What impediments will be found in the way of enlightening the people of Greece, cannot now be foreseen. It is hoped, however, that the establishment of schools, the circulation of the Bible, and other causes now in operation, will prepare the inhabitants to receive direct instruction in those things, which belong to their everlasting peace. The experience of Mr. [Jonas] King in missionary labors, the deep concern which he feels for the improvement of the people around the Mediterranean, and the interest excited by him personally in the minds and hearts of many Christians, in Europe and America, all conduce to the satisfaction of the Committee in numbering him among the missionaries and agents of the Board.

1831–1833
Report from the 22nd–24th Annual Meetings
No pertinent information

1834
Report from the 25th Annual Meeting
Reformed Dutch Church, Utica, New York
October 8–10, 1834

Pages 45–50

Mission to Constantinople — About midsummer of the present year, Messrs. Dwight and Schauffler made a tour in European Turkey, which they extended to Salonica, (anciently known by the name of Thessalonica,) and Adrianople. No particular account of their researches has yet been received. Their impressions were very favorable; and they recommend exploring Moldavia, Wallachia, and especially Servia.

1835

Report from the 26th Annual Meeting
First Presbyterian Church, Baltimore, Maryland
September 9–11, 1835

Pages 41–51
Tour in Macedonia and Thrace — This tour performed by Messrs. Dwight and Schauffler, was mentioned in the last report. A particular and valuable account of it has since been received. It was performed in the summer of last year. Our brethren visited Salonica, Seres, Pravista, the site of the ancient Philippi, Adrianople, and Rodosto. The last place had been visited by Mr. Dwight and Mr. Goodell, in their voyage round the sea of Marmora, in 1833. Salonica and Adrianople are recommended for missionary stations. Philippi, where the gospel was first planted in Europe, is desolate. ...

Salonica is recommended as a missionary station on account of its large population, its central position, the comparatively small expense of living, and because no permanent missionary of any society has ever yet settled in the place.

Adrianople is about forty-eight hours distant from the capital. Missionaries would there enjoy protection, and a station there would be a first step towards getting access to cities and countries beyond, which have not yet been explored by missionaries. One of these countries is Servia, which is said to be fast rising in civilization and intelligence. It is virtually independent of the Sultan, and is governed by its own prince, who is endeavoring to introduce European improvements. The other countries are Wallachia and Moldavia, now once more governed by Greek princes, and under the mutual protection of Turkey and Russia.

1836
Report from the 27th Annual Meeting
Central Church, Hartford, Connecticut
September 14–16, 1836

Pages 40–41
Europe, Mission to Greece
Athens — Jonas King, D.D., Missionary, and wife. Argos — Elias Riggs, Missionary, and wife. Nathan Benjamin, Missionary, and wife; on their way to the missions. *(2 stations, 3 missionaries, and 3 female assistant missionaries.)*

The prospects of substantial usefulness in this mission were perhaps never more encouraging than they are now. We are not indeed permitted to rejoice in view of the presence of the Holy Spirit to convert and sanctify the hearts of men; but the means of that mental illumination, which prepares the way for his gracious agency and usually precedes it, were never so rapidly and extensively diffused among the Greek people, as they have been the past year. Mr. King alone distributed by sale and gratuitously, during the year 1835, 2,656 copies of the New Testament and parts of the Old, in modern Greek, and 25,896 schoolbooks and religious tracts. These were distributed in the Peloponnesus, in continental Greece, in Joannini, Thessaly, Macedonia, and the islands; and he could, have disposed of many more had not his stock been exhausted. The schools of Greece, of which there are many, and the number is increasing, depend almost wholly on the presses of different missionary societies for their supply of books. It is not known that the government have yet published any books of this description, though a commissioner was appointed for this purpose soon after the arrival of the king. Lately the government has given Messrs. King and Riggs a formal permission to distribute books in all the villages of the kingdom.

1837–1841

Reports from the 28th–32nd Annual Meetings
No pertinent information

1842

Report from the 33rd Annual Meeting
Second Congregational Church, Norwich, Connecticut
September 13–16, 1842

Page 102
Europe, Mission to Turkey — Mr. Van Lennep has been perfecting himself in the Greek and Turkish languages, and mainly for this purpose has divided his time between Smyrna, Broosa, Constantinople and Adrianople. While at the place last named, he saw reason to believe that

missionary labors would be highly useful among the Bulgarians, a people professing the religion of the Greek Church. At a fair in the neighborhood of Adrianople, not less than 2,000 copies of the Bulgarian New Testament were sold.

Page 107
It is decided not to remove the seminary, which is under the care of Mr. Hamlin, to Smyrna. The school was first opened in apartments of an old decaying palace at Arnaout Keni, a village on the Bosphorus, six miles above Constantinople. This was in the summer of 1840. On the 4th of November it was removed to Bebeck, a mile above Arnaout Keni, where is the papal college mentioned in the last report.

1843
Report from the 34th Annual Meeting
No pertinent information

1844
Report from the 35th Annual Meeting
South Church, Worcester, Massachusetts
September 10–13, 1844

Pages 90–92
Europe, Mission to Greece — As good a view as can be given of the obstacles in the way of a successful mission among the Greeks, is contained in a late reply by Dr. King to an inquiry proposed by the Committee to the mission:

"What are the obstacles lying in the way of success?"

An obstacle is found also in their great and general antipathy to strangers. This antipathy they manifest, not only to those of other nations and languages, but to those of their own nation and their own language, from Constantinople, Epirus, and other places; even to those who have, for many years, been united with them, and fought in their battles for liberty. Now I consider this antipathy to strangers as very natural in a people that suffered so much from strangers, and which has in fact been governed by strangers for nearly twenty-two centuries—Romans, Venetians, Turks, Bavarians—none of whom perhaps ever sought their good to any great degree, either spiritual or temporal! "Surely oppression maketh a wise man mad"; and if the Greeks, in trying to throw off the yoke that has so long galled them, show a little madness and antipathy to strangers, I cannot wonder. I mention it only as an obstacle that exists in our way.

Under the Mussulman yoke, the Greek was taught from his childhood to regard every iota of his religion as most sacred; to suffer the greatest tortures and death itself, rather than renounce it; and he considers no disgrace, perhaps, in the eyes of his people so great, as to change his religion. The common people think, probably, that to correct errors which have gradually crept into the church, is the same as to change their religion, and renounce the Savior.

Page 97
Mr. Benjamin says, "Books distributed at the depot of Athens find their way into the following channels: The far greater number are given to schools ... the following schools were furnished with books from the depot at Athens from Jan. 1, 1842, to Nov. 30, 1843: ... In Turkey (Crete, Macedonia, Thessaly, &c.)—21 schools.

1845
Report from the 36th Annual Meeting
No pertinent information

1846
Report from the 37th Annual Meeting
Centre Church, New Haven, Connecticut
September 8–11, 1846

Pages 95–97
Western Asia, persecution and its results — The gratitude of the Christian world is due to the English Ambassador, Sir Stratford Canning, for his intelligent, impartial, and truly Christian course in relation to religious toleration in Turkey; in which he has been cordially aided by the Prussian Ambassador, Mr. Le Coq, by the American Minister, Mr. Carr, and by Mr. Brown, American Charge d'

Affaires in the absence of Mr. Carr. The British Minister has taken the lead in efforts to secure the freedom of religious opinions in Turkey. One of the older missionaries at the seat of government says:

> It matters not with him by what name the victim of persecution is called, or to what nation or denomination he belongs; whether he be Jew or Greek, Mohammedan, Armenian or Roman. This noble philanthropist is always ready to fly to his relief; and his influence in Turkey, I scarcely need inform you, is very great. The Lord has used him as an instrument in bringing about as great changes in this land as we have ever seen in any part of the world; and the recognition of the principle by this government that Protestant rayahs (subjects) can live in this country and pursue their lawful callings, and, at the same time, worship God according to the dictates of their consciences, is not among the least of these changes.

1847
Report from the 38th Annual Meeting
No pertinent information

1848

Report from the 39th Annual Meeting
Tremont Temple, Boston, Massachusetts
September 12–15, 1848

Pages 141–142

Western Asia, progress of toleration — The Lord has been the defender of his little flock in Turkey, and the plans and expectations of the enemy have thus far been disappointed. On the 15th of November, 1847, the Sultan's government formally recognized the Protestant subjects of the empire as constituting a separate and independent religious community. He has thus given to the brethren who compose the Evangelical Armenian churches, all the rights and privileges possessed by the most favored of the nominally Christian denominations in the empire. The following is the document.

> *Translation of an Order, obtained from the Sublime Porte by the Right Honorable Lord Cowley, in favor of the Sultan's Protestant subjects.*
>
> To His Excellency, the Pasha Comptroller of the City Revenue:
>
> Whereas the Christian subjects of the Ottoman Government, professing Protestantism, have experienced difficulty and embarrassment from not being hitherto under a special and separate jurisdiction, and naturally the Patriarch and the heads of the sects from which they have separated not being able to superintend their affairs;

and whereas it is in contravention to the supreme will of his Imperial Majesty our Gracious Lord and Benefactor, (may God increase him in years and power!) animated as he is with feelings of deep interest and clemency towards all classes of his subjects, that any of them should be subjected to grievance; and whereas the aforesaid Protestants, in conformity with the creed professed by them, do form a separate community: It is his Imperial Majesty's supreme will and command that for the sole purpose of facilitating their affairs, and of securing the welfare of said Protestants, the administration thereof should be henceforward confided to Your Excellency, together with the allotment of the taxes to which they are subjected by law; that you do keep a separate register of their births and deaths in the Bureau of your Department, according to the system observed with regard to the Latin subjects; that you do issue passports and permits of marriage; and that any person of established character and good conduct, chosen by them to appear as their agent at the Porte for the transaction and settlement of their current affairs, be duly appointed for that purpose. Such are the Imperial Commands, which you are to obey to the letter. But although passports and the allotment of taxes are placed under special regulations which cannot be infringed upon, you will be careful that, in pursuance of His Majesty's desire, no taxes be exacted from the Protestants for permits of marriage and registration; that any necessary assistance and facility be afforded to them in their current affairs; that no interference whatever be permitted in their temporal or spiritual concerns on the part of the Patriarch, monks or priests of other sects; but that they be enabled to exercise the profession of their creed in security, and that they be not molested one iota, either in that respect, or in any other way whatever.

(*Signed*) Reshid, Grand Vezir, November 15, 1847.

1849

Report from the 40th Annual Meeting
Tremont Temple, Pittsfield, Massachusetts
September 11–14, 1849

Page 64

When we mark the political changes which have taken place in Turkey and Persia; when we note the local relation which this mission holds to large portions of the unevangelized world; we cannot but expect the happiest results.

1850

Report from the 41st Annual Meeting
No pertinent information

1851

Report from the 42nd Annual Meeting
High Street Church, Portland, Maine
September 9–12, 1851

Pages 76–77

The report must not omit a grateful record of the fact, that the Protestant community has lately received a formal charter from the Imperial Government. For some three years or more there has been a vizierial recognition, and the complaints of the community have been listened to by the Porte; but it seems there was nothing which necessarily survived a change of administration. "The firman now obtained, being from the Sultan himself, and placed in their own hands, gives all the stability and permanency to their civil organization that the older Christian communities enjoy. They are distinctly declared to have the same privileges of building churches, holding burying grounds, &c., that are granted to the other rayahs (see a translation of the Firman in the Appendix).

Pages 224–225 (Appendix)
OFFICIAL CHARTER OF PROTESTANTS IN THE TURKISH EMPIRE

> To my Vizir, Mohammed Pasha, Prefect of the Police in Constantinople, the honorable Minister and glorious Counsellor, the Model of the world, and Regulator of the affairs of the community; who, directing the public interests with sublime prudence, consolidating the structure of the empire with wisdom, and strengthening

the columns of its prosperity and glory, is the recipient of every grace from the Most High. May God prolong his glory!

When this sublime and august mandate reaches you, let it be known, that hitherto those of my Christian subjects who have embraced the Protestant faith, in consequence of their not being under any specially appointed superintendence, and in consequence of the Patriarchs and primates of their former sects, which they have renounced, naturally not being able to attend to their affairs, have suffered much inconvenience and distress. But in necessary accordance with my imperial compassion, which is the support of all, and which is manifested to all classes of my subjects, it is contrary to my imperial pleasure that any one class of them should be exposed to suffering.

As therefore, by reason of their faith, the above mentioned are already a separate community, it is my royal compassionate will that for the facilitating the conducting of their affairs, and that they may obtain ease and quiet and safety, a faithful and trustworthy person from among themselves, and by their own selection, should be appointed, with the title of 'Agent of the Protestants,' and that he should be in relations with the Prefecture of the Police.

It shall be the duty of the Agent to have in charge the register of the male members of the community, which shall be kept at the police; and the Agent shall cause to be registered therein all births and deaths in the community. And all application for passports and marriage licenses, and all petitions on affairs concerning the community that are to be presented to the Sublime Porte, or to any other department, must be given in under the official seal of the Agent.

For the execution of my will, this my imperial sublime mandate and august command has been especially issued and given from my sublime chancery.

Hence thou who art the minister above named, according as it has been explained above, will execute to the letter the preceding ordinance; only, as the collection of the capitation tax and the delivery of passports are subject to particular regulations, you will not do any thing contrary to those regulations. You will not permit any thing to be required of them, in the name of fee, or on other pretences, for marriage licenses or registration. You will see to it, that like the other communities of the empire, in all their affairs, such as procuring cemeteries and places of worship, they should have every facility and every needed assistance. You will not permit that any of the other communities shall in any way interfere with their edifices, or with their worldly matters or concerns, or, in short, with any of their affairs, either secular or religious, that thus they may be free to exercise the usages of their faith.

And it is enjoined upon you not to allow them to be molested an iota in these particulars, or in any others; and that all attention and perseverance be put in requisition to maintain them in quiet and security. And, in case of necessity, they shall be free to make representations regarding their affairs through their Agent to the Sublime Porte.

When this my imperial will shall be brought to your knowledge and appreciation, you will have this august decree registered in the necessary departments, and then give it over to remain in the hands of these my subjects. And see you to it, that its requirements be always in future performed in their full import.

Thus know thou, and respect my sacred signet! Written in the holy month of Moharrem, 1267. (November, 1850.)

Given in the well guarded city Constantineniyeh.

1852

Report from the 43rd Annual Meeting
First Presbyterian Church, Troy, New York
September 7–10, 1852

Pages 58–59

Mission to the Jews — Last autumn, Mr. Parsons made a tour into Bulgaria, in company with Mr. Goldberg, of the London Jews' Society, then on his way from Salonica to his new station at Constantinople. Jews are found in most of the large places in Macedonia, Servia, Bosnia, Albania, Thessaly, Roumelia, and Bulgaria; to whom Salonica is the rabbinic, or religious, centre; and our brethren regard their duty as extending to the Jews residing in these districts. It was in the performance of this missionary duty that Mr. Parsons visited that part of Macedonia, which lies northwest of Salonica, and then extended his journey to Sophia, the capital of Bulgaria. In describing the country, Mr. Parsons says: "It lies principally between the Yardar and Struma, and presents almost every variety of scenery, extensive plains, mountains, hills, valleys, rivers, lakes and forests." "The whole region is more fully cultivated than Massachusetts, though with less skill and smaller returns. The chief productions are maize, wheat, rice, tobacco and cotton; the latter being raised extensively in the valley of the Struma." "Great quantities of Indian corn are shipped from Salonica to England."

Our missionary brethren commenced their tour Sept. 26th, with one of the Armenian helpers, a kavass from the Pasha for protection, and four horse-loads of Bibles. Their route lay through Doiran, situated among the mountains, on the west shore of a lake; Ostromja, in a magnificent valley watered by the ancient Pontus; Istip, a place of nearly five thousand houses; Koprili, upon three steep mountain slopes, with about five thousand houses, mostly Turkish; Scopia, on the head waters of the Yardar, mostly Turkish, with near four thousand houses. Thence they crossed hills and mountains covered with oak, beech and pine, the colors of the dying foliage almost equal in variety and brilliancy to those of New England; but there was no resemblance in the thatched huts, and the people were clothed from head to foot in sheepskins, with the wool outside. On the 14th of October, they arrived at Ghinstendil, the birthplace of Justinian, with twenty thousand souls, eighteen hundred of whom are supposed to be Jews. Four days later they crossed the Balkan, and entered Sophia, the capital of Bulgaria, containing a population of some thirty thousand Turks and Bulgarians, and at least six thousand Jews. Mr. Goldberg proceeded from this place to Constantinople, and Mr. Parsons returned to Salonica, where he arrived Oct. 30 (*Missionary Herald*, 1852, pp. 78–83). Much of the country through which they traveled is rich, and capable of supporting a dense population; but the inhabitants are generally poor, and between the church, the government, and the mountain robbers, there is little stimulus for the people to labor for anything beyond the bare necessaries of life. Much opposition was encountered from the ecclesiastics, who often succeeded in preventing the sale, to any great extent, of the Holy Scriptures. The eagerness of the people to possess them at Ghinstendil, burst through every obstacle, and Bibles enough were not left to satisfy their wants. ...

The Bulgarians —who shall send missionaries to them? "They are," says Mr. Dodd, "the *Armenians* of European Turkey. What began the reformation among the Armenians, but the same thirst for the word of God, which we see among the Bulgarians? There are about two hundred villages of this people scattered through Macedonia, besides numbers of them in Greek villages. These are more ignorant and less disposed to read, than those in Bulgaria, but they are simple hearted, and accessible to the missionary. In their own country, the Bulgarians are a reading people."

1853–1856

Reports from the 44th–47th Annual Meetings

No pertinent information

1857

Report from the 48th Annual Meeting
Beneficent Congregational Church, Providence, Rhode Island
September 8–11, 1857

Pages 61, 63, 65–66, 68

Mr. Clark has had the principal charge of the seminary at Bebek, during most of the year. The design is, as it has ever been, "to train a native agency for meeting the imperative wants of the mission; an agency, enlightened and Christianized, which may be employed with efficiency, for evangelizing and saving the people." ...

The average number of students during the year, has been forty-five; but the report states, "It has been with great difficulty and trial, that we have confined ourselves to such a limited number. Our prayers for more laborers have been signally answered. God has sent promising young men to us in scores. We have been entreated again and again to receive such. Good material has been urged upon us, that we might train it for Christ; but we have been compelled to say to many, 'We cannot receive you,' because the friends of the gospel have not given us the money to buy their bread." Sixty applicants, within the year, were thus rejected, though "with the same board of instruction, and with the present classification of pupils, one hundred could receive instruction in the seminary, as easily as fifty." "Numerous applications have we had for admission into our seminary from Bulgarians, Albanians, Wallachians, and Servians; but we had no provision for their training, and they could not be received."

In European Turkey — Still larger and more urgent are the demands in the west. In April and May, before the annual meeting of the mission, Dr. Hamlin accompanied the Rev. Henry Jones, Traveling Secretary of the Turkish Missions Aid Society in England, on a tour of exploration from Constantinople to Rodosto, Adrianople and Philippopolis, with special reference to the Bulgarians, whom Mr. Jones had been requested by his Society to visit.

Bulgaria, on the maps, is a country between the Danube and the Balkan mountains, which may be considered as a continuation of the Alps, south-eastward, between the waters of the Adriatic and the Danube, and reaching the Black Sea near Yarna; but the Bulgarians consider it as including a large and indefinite extent of country south of the Balkan, over which they are diffused. Even on the way from Rodosto to Adrianople, the explorers say, "Wherever we saw flocks, we saw Bulgarian shepherds; and wherever we saw cultivation, we saw Bulgarian laborers. They are indeed spread all over Roumelia as laborers and shepherds, and the industry of the country is in their hands." ...

Leaving Philippopolis May 9, the travelers reached Constantinople before the annual meeting, and Dr. Hamlin reported to the following effect:

1. The field, a part of which we have surveyed, is peculiarly accessible and compact. No long and painful journeys are required to reach any part of it. When we extend our labors into Servia, Bosnia, and Hertzgowina, we can reach them not only from Philippopolis, but from the Danube and the Adriatic; and there is a strong probability that ere long railroads will pass through the central regions. From Bourgas, Adrianople, Philippopolis, Kustendil, Uscup, (Scopia,) Monastir, and Seres, a population of between one and two millions of Bulgarians and Moslems can be approached, and the native agency for evangelizing them directed and controlled.

2. It is a population earnestly calling for the word of God. No unevangelized people ever purchased the Bible with such eagerness as the Bulgarians.

3. Much of the preparatory work is already done. The Bible for the Bulgarians is mostly translated, and is waiting Mr. Higgs's return. The Bible Society is ready for active and efficient measures to circulate it as soon as printed. The great question of freedom of conscience has been worked out for the whole empire. There may be some peculiar difficulties in its application to European Turkey, but we are not to hesitate a moment in claiming it as a principle of universal application. All our missionary experience also goes into this field, and will enable us to advance boldly where, without such experience, we should hesitate or retreat.

4. The Bulgarian population have such a desire for schools, for the cultivation of their own language, and for freedom from Greek despotism, that they will be disposed to receive the assistance which otherwise they might reject. They generally regard the Greek yoke as more insupportable than that of the Turks. They are now engaged in a fierce contest, on the basis of the Hatti-Sherif, for those obvious rights which other nationalities enjoy.

5. This will be an expensive mission. It has opened upon us suddenly. It will not require, like the Armenian mission, long years of preparatory labor to open the doors; they are already open. A great and extensive native agency is to be raised up upon the soil, for which the first school and the first school-book does not exist. The true missionary principle is to give the gospel, with all its blessings, to each nation in its own spoken language, and to commit the treasure to an educated native ministry. Our whole experience in Western Asia shows, that no one institution can do this, but every central place must be provided with its own schools, and the whole apparatus of a Christian education. Adrianople, Philippopolis, Scopia, Monastir, etc., must be regarded as centres from which is to go forth a native agency, in schools, colportage, and preaching, while a central institution shall be preparing a more thoroughly trained agency, to follow up the work. All this will require a large outlay from the beginning, and the larger it is, the more profitable will be the investment.

In view of the magnitude of the work, as it expands before us, we rejoice in the prospect of its being carried on by the united efforts of English and American Christians. It is an enterprise which will give new life and power to the missionary cause, in all the Christian churches engaged in it.

Prospects of Toleration — With these prospects before us, the question inevitably recurs with new interest, how far can we rely upon the execution, by the Turkish Government, of its late edict in favor of religious liberty?

1858
Report from the 49th Annual Meeting
First Presbyterian Church, Detroit, Michigan
September 7–10, 1858

Pages 46–48
Methodist Bulgarian Mission — The station at Adrianople, commenced this year as the beginning of missionary labor among the Bulgarians ... Here it seems proper to notice the commencement of the American Methodist mission to the Bulgarians. .... It was determined that Mr. Prettyman should establish himself at Varna, and Mr. Long at Shumla. The importance of the places selected is well known, as all travel between the valley of the Danube and European Turkey, whether for military, commercial, or other purposes, naturally seeks to pass the Balkan range at Shumla, or turn it at Varna. These advantages of position may prove as valuable in a missionary, as in

a military campaign. Mr. Bliss was inclined to rank the Bulgarians above the Armenians in native intelligence and in cultivation. Our brethren desire the arrangement of a boundary between the field of this mission and their own.

1859
Report from the 50th Annual Meeting
First Presbyterian Church, Philadelphia, Pennsylvania
October 4–7, 1859

Pages 60–61

European Turkey as a field for Missions

The population of European Turkey is thus stated by Dr. Dwight: Romanians, 4,000,000; Slavonians, 7,500,000; Proper Greeks, 1,000,000; Albanians, 1,500,000; Osmanly Jews, 1,000,000; Armenians, Jews, and others, 500,000; Total, 15,500,000.

The Osmanly Turks are less than a fifteenth of the whole population. There are probably four millions of Mohammedans, but at least three-fourths of them are of Christian origin. A large portion of the Albanians have professed the Mohammedan religion, multitudes of the Bulgarians have done the same, and so, especially, have the Bosnians. The so-called Turkish rulers of Bosnia speak the language of the country, and belonged originally to the Slavonian race. Though they insist on being called Turks, and make a show of great zeal for Mohammedanism, yet they sometimes secretly employ Greek priests to bless the remains of their dead, and to pray for the departed souls of their friends. The Osmanly Turks are not only few, but, from their position and circumstances, they must be far less bigoted than their fellow-countrymen and co-religionists in Asiatic Turkey. Having been born and educated on the very borders of Europe, and in the midst of divers Christian races, of a peculiarly independent spirit, their characters must be formed on a different model from that of the true Asiatic Turk. By far the greater part of the Christian races profess the Greek religion, though, as has been seen, only about one million, out of eleven millions, are true and proper Greeks. Most of them are of Slavonian or Tartar origin, and they cherish the most perfect dislike to the Greek bishops, whose policy always has been, and is, to extinguish, if possible, every remnant of national feeling, and obliterate all traces of their real origin. A constant struggle has been going on, for a long time, between these races and the Greek Patriarch and his bishops; and the oppressed and down-stricken people would hail, as their greatest benefactors, any kind friends from abroad who should come to their aid. Of all the races now mentioned, the Bulgarians undoubtedly claim our first attention.

1860

Report from the 51st Annual Meeting
Tremont Temple, Boston, Massachusetts
October 2–5, 1860

Page 48

European Turkey and Western Asia — The name of this mission [Northern Armenian Mission] has become inappropriate. Its labors are now demanded for other races, besides the Armenians. Three stations in European Turkey are especially for the benefit of the Bulgarians; and not only at the capital, but in other parts of its wide field, we are called to care for the Moslems. Thus, in fulfillment of its original design, has this mission to Oriental Christians, also grown into a mission to Mohammedans. Extending from the Balkans to the eastern head-waters of the Euphrates, it embraces too large a territory. The mission has therefore recommended, that the eastern stations and the Assyrian mission constitute a distinct mission, to be called "The Mission to Eastern Turkey"; and the remaining stations are to receive the designation of "The Mission to Western Turkey."

Pages 59–61

The Bulgarians — According to the careful estimates of Drs. Dwight and Hamlin, the number of Bulgarians in European Turkey is about four millions. This is less than the population which they claim for themselves, and which is given to them by some standard authorities.

With the exception of a few localities, where Greek is spoken, the Bulgarian language is the one used by all classes of the people. Belonging to the Greek church, they are under the Patriarch of Constantinople; their clergy are mostly Greek, and that language is the one of their church services. An earnest contest is going on between the people and the clergy, the demand of the former being relief from ecclesiastical oppression, and the use of the national language in schools and religious worship. Mr. Meriam writes from Philippopolis, that this struggle for independence of Greek rule portends a revolution, if it is not granted. The people welcome Protestant aid, not from a sense of spiritual want, but from a desire for civil, intellectual and social elevation. They eagerly receive the Scriptures; and the missionaries are treated with great friendliness by the people, though opposed by the ecclesiastics. ...

Eski Zagra is seventy-five miles northwest from Adrianople, sixty north-east from Philippopolis, and twenty miles south of the Balkan mountains. It lies at the northern extremity of a beautiful plain, surrounded by a country of extraordinary fertility. It has a population of 10,000 Bulgarians, 8,000 Turks, and a few Jews. "There are in the town," writes Mr. Byington, "six Bulgarian schools for boys, with eight hundred scholars; and four schools for girls, with one hundred and thirty-five scholars. In the surrounding villages there are eleven schools, with three hundred scholars. For their two principal schools they have two fine, spacious buildings, which would not disgrace even a New England town. The teachers are very gentlemanly men, and manifest much enthusiasm for their work. The higher class of Bulgarian teachers have generally received their education abroad, and Russia seems to be their favorite place. This may arise chiefly from the fact, that they can secure an education there without expense. These teachers are the men of influence, and they are earnest in their efforts to introduce a higher civilization. The spirit they are now manifesting in preparing and publishing school books, reflects honor upon the Bulgarian name and nation. With them it is no money-making operation, but the contrary; and thus it must continue to be for some time to come; but the books are needed, and therefore they exert themselves. And it is by them that we have everywhere received the most cordial welcome. How different the character of the priests."

The efforts of the metropolitan bishop to prevent Mr. Byington's access to the people, were defeated. "Scarcely a day has passed," he remarks, "without a visit from some one, and to some we have been enabled to preach Christ and him crucified, in the plainest manner."

The Bulgarian department needs to be strengthened. Its beginning is promising.

1861
Report from the 52nd Annual Meeting
No pertinent information

1862

52nd Annual Report
City Hall, Springfield, Massachusetts
October 7–10, 1862

Editorial Note (D.H., 2017): This report was actually the fifty-third year of reporting, but it was considered the fifty-second report, likely because two of the early years had been combined into one report. The reports through 1861 had been titled simply "The Report of the ABCFM," with the year of the publication. In 1862 the report titles began to include the number of the report. In 1862, therefore, the annual report was entitled "The Fifty-Second Report." The 1863 report was called the "Fifty-Third Report," and so on.

Pages 80–81

Western Turkey — The mission has been authorized to commence a boarding school for males, and another for females, among the Bulgarians — the former to be at Philippopolis, and the latter at Eski Zagra. The Bulgarians have been rendered less impressible by evangelical truth through their long connection with the Greek Church, and recently through zealous efforts of the Church of Rome; and such schools are thought to be among the necessary incipient measures for gaining access to them. The schools are to be commenced on a small scale. There are already eleven pupils at Philippopolis.

1863

53rd Annual Report
Brick Church, Rochester, New York
October 6–9, 1863

Pages 63–64

Bulgarian Stations — The work among the Bulgarians, while not answering the expectations entertained a few years since by some, is making progress. ...

1864

54th Annual Report
Mechanics' Hall, Worcester, Massachusetts
October 4–7, 1864

Pages 13–17

Recent Events in Turkey (persecution) — The committee on the Missions to Western and Central Turkey, respectfully represent ... the recent remarkable acts of the Turkish Government, in seizing the presses and closing the bookstore of our mission, and arresting and casting into prison certain of its own subjects, who were guilty of no other offense than that of exercising, in accordance with the laws of the empire, the religion of their choice ...

Page 59

Western Turkey — The field of the mission to Western Turkey, includes European Turkey south of the Balkan range of mountains, and Asia Minor west of 38° east longitude. It embraces three distinct nationalities—the Armenians, the Bulgarians, and the Turks,—upon which the efforts of the mission are bestowed. ...

Pages 71–72
The Bulgarian Field — The struggle of the Bulgarians for an ecclesiastical independence is still unsuccessful. The national unity which they seek would probably become a greater obstacle to the introduction of the gospel, and God does not allow them to gain it.

Dr. Riggs has carried on his revision of the Bulgarian Scriptures through about one-half of the New Testament. In this work he has the aid of two efficient native translators, representing different dialects of the language, and latterly has had the valuable co-operation of Rev. A. L. Long, of the American Methodist Episcopal mission. By this joint labor, the version is made one that it is believed will be generally acceptable to the people, and become a permanent standard of the language. A small monthly paper, called the "Morning Star," edited by Mr. Long, has met an unexpectedly welcome reception and promises to be very useful. It was warmly recommended by the Bulgarian national newspaper. The circulation of tracts and books has gone forward against some opposition, but with evidence of good results. The awakening of the Bulgarians on the subject of education is indicated by the multiplication of schools. ...

The Mussulmans in European Turkey are generally more friendly and accessible to foreigners than they are in Asia. The missionaries among the Bulgarians have favorable opportunities for intercourse with them; and this department of the mission deserves to be supported vigorously, in view of its relations not only to the Bulgarians and the Slavic nations, but also to the ultimate aim of our work among the oriental Christians, with reference to the Mohammedan populations.

1865
55th Annual Report
No pertinent information

1866
56th Annual Report
First Congregational Society, Pittsfield, Massachusetts
September 25–28, 1866

Pages 15–20
Committee on the Western Turkey Mission — While the Armenian mind is becoming more and more interested in the truth, a change for the better, giving promise of a new order of things, would seem to have commenced among the Bulgarians. Their former indifference has yielded to a spirit of inquiry. The missionary brethren among them are greatly encouraged; and no longer confining themselves, as they have heretofore for the most part done, to

the schools, as the only means of reaching the people, they are giving more and more of their time to the work of preaching at the stations and in the surrounding country.

The great want of this interesting missionary field is, as heretofore, that of more laborers to gather in the ripening harvest. ...

The American Board and the American Methodist Episcopal Society divide between them the Bulgarian field in Turkey.

Page 72
The Bulgarians — The most discouraging feature of the work for some years past, among this people, has been the almost total want of a spirit of inquiry. Testaments were sold by the hundred, but there was no evidence that they were thoughtfully read. The people seemed utterly indifferent. The past year has witnessed the beginning of what it is hoped will be a great change. Mr. Byington writes that "error no longer reigns with undisputed sway. Here and there a voice is heard disputing its claims and resisting its pretensions. The thick darkness which has so long brooded over the land is being relieved by the first faint rays of morning light." Similar testimony is given by others. The patient continuance in well doing, on the part of the servants of Christ, is beginning to bear fruit. The number who are ready to listen to the preaching of the Word is increasing. The work of the Spirit, hitherto confined in great measure to the girls' boarding school at Eski Zagra, is beginning to reach the young men in the

school at Philippopolis also; and no objection is made to the free instruction of the youth who attend our schools in the truths of the Gospel. In the tours that are made to the villages about the stations, there is found a readiness to converse and to listen to the Gospel as never before.

1867
57th Annual Report
No pertinent information

1868
58th Annual Report
Broadway Congregational Church, Norwich, Connecticut
October 6–9, 1868

Pages xvi–xvii
Remarks from the Committee on Missions to Western Turkey and Greece — With respect to the missions to Western Turkey, we notice that notwithstanding the great changes among missionary laborers in this field, the measures adopted for the self-support of the churches have met with encouraging success; the number of the pupils in the seminaries is increasing; the prospect is hopeful of raising up a native ministry to supply the wants of the churches; the press is furnishing, rapidly, a Christian literature; the wives of missionaries, together with native helpers, are carrying their elevating influence among the

women; and an almost unexampled spirit of benevolence is awakened in some of the churches.

1869
59th Annual Report
Third Presbyterian Church, Pittsburgh, Pennsylvania
October 5–8, 1869
No pertinent information

1870
60th Annual Report
Academy of Music, Brooklyn, New York
October 4–7, 1870

Page 12

The missions in Turkey — Exclusive of Syria, the operations of the Board in the Turkish Empire are carried on through the organizations known as the Western, Central, and Eastern Turkey missions. These divisions are simply for convenience of administration. They include the portion of European Turkey south and east of the Balkan Mountains, the whole of Asia Minor, and Eastern provinces, to the border of the field occupied by the mission to Persia, and on the south to a line running beyond Antioch and Aleppo in Syria, and Mosul in Mesopotamia.

Page 22

Western Turkey — At the last annual meeting of the Western Turkey mission, it was resolved to recommend the organization of a separate mission for this field. Accordingly the Eski Zagra, Philippopolis, Samokov, and Adrianople stations, and including Dr. Riggs, of Constantinople, whose labors are chiefly for the Bulgarians, will be constituted the mission to European Turkey. Mr. Schauffler will join the Philippopolis station, where he will use the Turkish and Greek languages for the benefit of the populations speaking them; and the work among Bulgarians will everywhere be made to connect itself, as fast and as far as may be practicable, with that for Mohammedans and Greeks with whom they are intermingled.

The gaining of ecclesiastical independence by the Bulgarians is followed by the anticipated effect of a stronger national spirit, and a greater unwillingness to allow Protestantism to come in as an element of division. Few of the people can see how a man can be a Bulgarian and a Protestant at the same time. It is evident that no general movement, and no leaning, on the part of rulers and ecclesiastics, toward Protestantism, is to be expected. But a desire for education increases. The circulation of the Scriptures and evangelical publications can be carried on. In quiet modes, much may be done to disseminate a knowledge of the way of life, and to reach thoughtful minds burdened with a sense of sin and of the wants of the soul. Examples of what the gospel can do to regenerate character and give peace are beginning to attract attention; and the nucleus of an evangelical church has begun to form. ...

Samokov is more healthful, and a better centre than Sophia. Messrs. Locke and Page find much encouragement in this district. A merchant of Samokov is an active convert and very influential. At Bansko a religious movement of great promise has been inaugurated. It is expected that a church will soon be organized there.

The seed sown in the Bulgarian field is beginning everywhere to spring up. With the Divine blessing on continued and enlarged labor, an abundant harvest will yet be reaped.

1871

61st Annual Report
Mechanics Hall, Salem, Massachusetts
October 3–6, 1871

Pages 14–18
European Turkey Mission — The little company of missionaries who have hitherto been laboring in the Bulgarian language, as a part of the Western Turkey Mission, have now been set off as a separate mission, to do the work of evangelization for European Turkey.

Female Boarding School — As the quarters occupied by the boarding-school have become too narrow for it, and some change has thus been rendered necessary, it has seemed advisable to the mission to remove the school altogether from Eski Zagra to Samokov, both on account of the greater healthfulness of the latter place, and the much greater facilities afforded there for securing suitable buildings. It is expected that this decision will be carried into effect as soon as suitable arrangements can be made for the school at Samokov.

Constantinople — So far as this mission is concerned, Constantinople is simply a point from which the Scriptures and tracts can be conveniently issued and circulated over the whole land. Dr. Riggs has occasionally preached in Bulgarian, but his labors have been mostly in the line of literary work.

Samokov — A regular Sabbath service has been held by the missionaries at Samokov during the year, and a weekly prayer meeting has been held at the houses of the native Christians. Three new houses have of late opened their doors to this meeting, and thus some have heard the truth for the first time. Though the audiences at these services are as yet very small, it was reported at the annual meeting of the mission that there were five persons there deemed worthy to be received to church fellowship.

The field and its wants — European Turkey is occupied by a population estimated at from twelve to fourteen millions, of whom five or six millions are Bulgarians. The remainder are mostly Turks and Greeks, the Armenians being confined chiefly to Constantinople and its vicinity. This is far the most advanced and civilized portion of the Turkish Empire. ...

More than forty Bulgarian young men are found among the students of Robert College. Throughout the land are men eager to search into the truth of every new doctrine; and as they shake off the influence of their old superstitions, they may be led, with almost equal ease, into truth or error ...

In this wide and most inviting field only pioneer work has as yet been done, and that only among the Bulgarians. No churches have been organized, though here and there converts have been received to Christian communion. But the missionaries have thoroughly explored the field, have become acquainted with its wants, have fixed upon strategic points that should be occupied, and in all respects are ready to move vigorously forward, if only the needed reinforcements can be sent them.

1872

62nd Annual Report
Music Hall, New Haven, Connecticut
October 1–4, 1872

Pages 9–13
European Turkey Mission — A church was organized, with fifteen members, at the out-station Bansko, and

a pastor ordained, in August, 1871, with encouraging prospects. "This was the first church formed, and the first pastor ordained, by this mission," and the day was one of joy and gratitude. Seven members have been added since the organization, giving the church a present membership of twenty-two. There is an average Sabbath congregation at Bansko of eighty-five; it has reached one hundred and ten. The church seems to be spiritually growing, and "many of the villages around are feeling its influence" ...

Dr. Riggs, of Constantinople, reports of his work for the year, so far as it was specially for this mission: "The only publication issued has been the Hymn Book, 154 pages, 5,000 copies; total, 770,000 pages, 16mo. Our first little collection of hymns in Bulgarian was issued in 1862, and contained twenty-five hymns. The Hymn and Tune Book, published in 1866, contained eighty Bulgarian hymns (eighty-one, including one re-written,) and twenty Turkish hymns in Bulgarian characters. It is, therefore, with some degree of satisfaction, and with hopeful feelings as to its spiritual influence, that we now issue this collection of one hundred and forty Bulgarian hymns, most of them translations from some of our most precious English hymns."[1]

Educational — In accordance with plans announced last year, the female boarding-school has been removed from

---

[1] The first Albanian hymn books (*Kënkë të Sentëruara*, 1906, and *Këngë të Shenjtëruara*, 1927) were translated by various Albanians from Bulgarian, English and Greek, and prepared by Gjergj Qiriazi (George Kyrias) (DH).

Eski Zagra to Samokov, where it was opened in September, 1871....

The mission reiterates its call for enlargement. "It is thought desirable to establish, as soon as possible, a new station in Macedonia, and in case of the North Balkan field coming into our hands, to establish one or two stations in that section." .... "We need at once three men for the new station in Macedonia: one to reinforce Messrs. Haskell and Bond at Eski Zagra; and if you should at once send us six for the North Balkan field, it is probable that their places would be ready for them before they could get here, and be ready for the work."

1873

63rd Annual Report
Academy of Music, Minneapolis, Minnesota
September 23–26, 1873

Pages 10–13

European Turkey Mission — On the 5th of October, 1872, the day after the meeting of this Board closed at New Haven, three young men, Messrs. Marsh, Baird, and House, the latter with his wife, sailed from New York to reinforce this mission. They reached Eski Zagra November 27, where they have been specially engaged in the study of the language, while becoming acquainted with, and aiding as they could, in the details of missionary work. The interest felt by one at least of these brethren in the work for which they went abroad, is indicated in a letter from Mr. Marsh, written after they had been some months in the field. He remarks: —

> I suppose I may properly consider my missionary experience as beginning when I entered European Turkey; at least I had unspeakable delight. Of course I saw from the first the sad effects of misrule, and a false or dead faith. But I was assured that God had purposes of mercy towards this people, and that He would not delay them long. Was it because I saw everything ideally — because I saw the capabilities of this land and people — that I embraced all their interests so heartily, and consecrated myself to the work so joyfully?
>
> I have been with Brother Bond on two trips of five days each ... To see a native brother open his house for the service, and the people come in by scores to listen and see, is encouraging. It incites one to hasten his preparation to enter upon the work. Oh for a tongue to speak the language of the people! As I looked at them, joining in our songs of praise and giving reverent attention, and saw the few confessing Christ, even though it means persecution for them, I could feel the blood quickening in its course through my veins. I try not to be in too great haste, but it is hard to learn that nothing is more heroic than patience. My tongue is restless till I can preach the gospel in Bulgarian.

At the recent meeting of the mission, steps were taken looking to the establishment of another station in Macedonia, to be occupied by Messrs. Marsh, Baird, and Jenney.

Seminaries, books — On the 11th of September, 1872, a theological school was opened at Samokov, with eleven pupils, six of whom had previously been connected with a station class at Eski Zagra. ... Nearly all the students are said to exhibit serious earnestness in preparing themselves for future work, and in using present opportunities for making Christ known among the people. They have had "a bi-monthly recess of six days, for missionary work," all entering cordially upon the plan, and have gone out, two by two, to neighboring places. Twenty different places have been visited in this way, from once to four times each, while special work has been done also in the city. Thus, it is said, "a good beginning has been made in the Theological Seminary." In the boarding-school for girls, at Samokov, there have been 29 pupils.

1874

64th Annual Report
Congregational Church, Rutland, Vermont
October 6–9, 1874

Pages 8–10
European Turkey Mission — The reports from the stations of this mission show encouraging progress. ... The press has continued to send forth tracts, books, and the monthly numbers of the *Zornitza* ("Morning Star"), at Constantinople, under the direction of Dr. Riggs. So much of Dr. Riggs' time is now given to the new edition of the Turkish Scriptures

that the mission earnestly calls for a competent man, who shall reside at Constantinople and take charge of the "Morning Star," and of the work of the press in Bulgaria ... The new station at Monastir was first occupied by Messsrs. Baird and Jenney, and their wives, and Mr. Marsh in October, 1873. "Monastir was chosen as the place of residence because of its healthfulness, and because it is not only the governmental center, but also, to some extent, a commercial center. From this place missionary work can be prosecuted in the Greek, Turkish, and Albanian languages." The first annual report of the station shows that all the missionaries have given the greater part of their time and strength to the study of the Bulgarian language. A service conducted by a native helper was begun soon after the arrival of the missionaries, the attendance on which gradually increased to sixty persons. But many of these doubtless came from curiosity, and the number soon fell off until it was only "from five to twenty-five." A Wednesday evening prayer-meeting has been regularly maintained.

1875

65th Annual Report
Farwell Hall, Chicago, Illinois
October 5–8, 1875

Page 14

European Turkey Mission, Monastir — The curious crowds which at first thronged the chapel at Monastir, are reported as having found the Word too pointed and too destructive to favorite plans in life, and as having, little by little, left; but the missionaries rejoice more in the present few who, Bible in hand, study the Word of God. A Sabbath-school has been commenced, which seemed to be just the thing demanded for awakening, encouraging, and assisting a desire to study the Bible. From fifteen to twenty-five are regular in attendance on each Sabbath service, and a few have so far overcome superstition as to work on saints' days. "The New Testament is found in the pockets of many, and the discussions in the market, as to the relative merits of the Greek and the Protestant faith, are long and warm." Mrs. Baird and her servant have made weekly visits to a circle of women, for the purpose of reading and explaining the Scriptures. Much time has been necessarily spent by the brethren at this station in the study of the language; yet sixty-five days have been employed by them in touring, and forty-three by the helper. Their report closes by saying: "We live in the hope that some souls will soon rejoice in the new experience of Christ's love."

1876

66th Annual Report
Robert's Opera House, Hartford, Connecticut
October 3–6, 1876

Page 14

European Turkey Mission, Monastir — Letters from Mr. Jenney, of the Monastir station, some of which have appeared in the "Missionary Herald" within the year (in January, April, June, and September), indicate that he has met with much encouragement in direct, personal efforts to reach the minds and hearts of the people, upon tours, and at the station. ...

1877

67th Annual Report
Music Hall, Providence, Rhode Island
October 2, 1877

Pages 17–19

European Turkey Mission, Condition of the Empire — The public mind has been greatly disturbed by the anxieties attendant on the political situation. In the early part of the past year, the insurrection in a portion of this field, and its suppression with great cruelty, interrupted missionary operations to some extent, and at a later date drew off a number of the missionaries from their distinctive work to labors in behalf of the sufferers. Mr. Clarke gave over six months of his time in connection with a relief committee, and joined with Lady Strangford, and others from Great Britain, in supplying the destitute with necessary means of living and otherwise ministering to the necessities of the distressed people. ...

The new station at Monastir also reports progress, in the larger attendance upon public worship, and in the greater readiness to listen to the gospel. It would seem that the political situation, and the anxieties attending thereon, have led not a few to turn their thoughts away from all earthly reliances, and to seek rest and help in the gospel of Christ. Instances are given of faithful, devoted labor on the part of those who have recently become acquainted with the truth. One of these, an ex-priest, is doing a good work in his own village. Many who were bitterly opposed to him a year ago are now eager listeners to the truth from his lips. A good beginning has been made at this point.

1878

68th Annual Report
Immanuel Presbyterian Church, Milwaukee, Wisconsin
October 1–4, 1878

Pages 24–27

European Turkey Mission — Much of the field of this mission was the seat of war, violence, outrage, and terrible suffering for a large part of the year to be now reported. No annual meeting has been held by the mission, no mission reports, and no full station reports or statistics, have been received; but some facts in regard to the several stations may be gathered from the correspondence. ...

Monastir — From the latter part of November, 1877, to May, 1878, Mr. and Mrs. Baird were without associates at Monastir. Before Mr. Jenney left, the brethren had written of the prospects in that field as on the whole encouraging. The attendance on Sabbath services had increased to from 30 to 40 adults in the morning, and from 20 to 30 in the afternoon, opposition had "well-nigh passed away," and young converts seemed to "grow in grace, knowledge, and devotion." The country around was quiet and excited by turns. Eleven persons are reported as added to the church at that station, and two at an outstation. Mr. Jenney wrote after his return from the excitement and perils of the winter at Samokov: "I felt as if I had reached an earthly paradise last Sabbath, as I gazed on the happy, earnest faces of an audience drinking in the words of life. I rejoice more and more that I came to Turkey, and that I came to Monastir."

1879

69th Annual Report
Plymouth Congregational Church, Syracuse, New York
October 7, 1879

Page 19

European Turkey Mission, Monastir — A steady growth has been observed in the Protestant community in this city. Forty or more attend preaching services on the Sabbath, while none who have regularly attended hitherto have been obliged to go elsewhere for means of subsistence. The missionaries are especially encouraged by the work among the women. A native Bible helper, Marika, educated in the Seminary at Samokov, has been engaged at Monastir as a teacher and Bible reader. She and Mrs. Jenney have shared special labors in behalf of women, going to separate places where they have read and explained the Word of God to many. The result is a large attendance of women on religious services, and the fact that many are now beginning to read in order to study the Scriptures for themselves. This feature is the more hopeful because the greatest hindrance hitherto has been found in the ignorance of the women. There are few men who openly oppose, but the women have been especially bitter in their opposition. No report of the station can give an adequate view of what has really been accomplished. The result of conversation in the market-places, of personal interviews with inquirers, cannot be given in statistics, though the missionaries look forward to gathering fruit from such labors in time to come. In consequence of the disturbed condition of the country less touring has been done than usual, though it is believed that in several out-stations, as the result of such efforts as have been made, many have become enlightened, and only wait for further instruction to take a decided stand on the side of the truth."

1880
70th Annual Report
Huntington Hall, Lowell, Massachusetts
October 5–8, 1880

Pages 31–35

European Turkey Mission — The four stations of this mission are now under three distinct governments, but their efforts are mainly for the Bulgarians. The people of this race are by no means confined to the Principality of Bulgaria. Yet they all speak the Bulgarian language, and it is in this tongue that the missionaries are proclaiming the gospel in Macedonia and Eastern Roumelia, as well as in Bulgaria proper.

Monastir — The year at this station has been one of sowing rather than of reaping. It is the only station of the Board in Macedonia, and the two missionaries who occupy this post have spent one hundred and sixty-one days in touring. At Yatasha, the one out-station, a preacher is located, and a bookseller, who has been at work most of the year. The latter has found much encouragement, notwithstanding the hard times and the high price of food. At Perlepe and Resen the missionaries have had good and attentive audiences, and a friendly spirit has been shown on the part of the people. In Monastir itself there has been about the usual attendance at the public services, but the missionaries deplore the lack of unity and Christian fellowship among the people. There are signs, however, of a better state of things at hand. The girls' school, which had dwindled in numbers during the summer, opened in the autumn with an attendance of from sixteen to twenty-six. In the judgment of the mission this school should be made a boarding school, and should be placed upon a permanent basis, like the girls' school at Samokov. There is a call, also, for a third missionary at this station, inasmuch as the Macedonian field, of which it is the center, is large enough to cover several New England States and cannot properly be worked with the present force. ...

In no part of the great mission field have the labors of missionaries told so immediately and so powerfully upon the intellectual and political life of the people, as in European Turkey. The men trained in the mission schools and brought most fully under mission influence, are in the greatest request, to be leaders in the social and political movements of the time, and especially because of the confidence felt in their integrity.

The following tribute to the services of the American Missionaries among the Bulgarians, from the pen of the Marquis of Bath, in a recent volume entitled "Observations on Bulgarian Affairs," will be of interest to the friends of the American Board: —

> If the [Bulgarian] nation rises again to spiritual life, its recovery will be in no small degree owing to the intellectual and devotional influence and example of a small and devoted company of American missionaries, who abandoned homes in their own land for the purpose of promoting the welfare of an uncared-for and oppressed people—alone of all the missionary bodies regardless of the political influence of their own country, or of the interests of any particular sect. If the list of their converts is not a large one—and perhaps it is well that it should be small—their work in raising the moral tone of the nation, and in aiding the regeneration of its ancient church, will not have been less important.
>
> The American missionaries have contributed in no small degree to foster the spirit of toleration among the Bulgarian people. Carefully abstaining from any interference in political questions, they have thrown no impediment in the way of their converts joining the patriotic movement, which numbers some of them among its leaders. They have aroused the jealousy and excited the suspicions of no political party. In the darkest times of Turkish rule they relieved the needy and succored the oppressed. No religious test has been imposed on admission into their schools; and there is hardly a town in Bulgaria where persons are not to be found who owe to them the advantages of a superior education. The result of their teaching has permeated all Bulgarian society, and is not the least important of the

causes that have rendered the people capable of wisely using the freedom so suddenly conferred upon them.

1881

71st Annual Report
Pilgrim Church, St. Louis, Missouri
October 18–21, 1881

Pages 29–31

European Turkey Mission — This mission has pursued its work hopefully, and its expanding opportunities for labor call for more reenforcement than it has received. ...

The American Collegiate and Theological Institute at Samokov—despite some embarrassing changes—reports a measure of prosperity which fills the mission with gratitude and joy. The new building was occupied at the beginning of the year. It has a room for the philosophical apparatus, and another devoted to the library and museum. ... Forty students have been in attendance during the year, four in the Theological class, ten each in the first and third classes, and sixteen in the second. Of this number, thirteen are professors of the Protestant faith. ...

Monastir reports the removal of difficulties and decided progress. Four have been received to communion, representing three nationalities, two Bulgarians, one Albanian, and one Gypsy, the latter giving witness of the change by the tithes paid to the Lord. Bitter persecution is a thing of the past; still the shame of changing one's faith, and the ridicule of priests, deter many from publicly accepting that which conscience affirms to be the word of God. The Protestants, by intellectual conviction, can be numbered by hundreds in Macedonia. The most serious hindrance to the spread of the gospel is the superstitious ignorance of the women. There are schools for boys in all large places, but the girls are principally taught fancy work. The mixture in them of ignorance and superstition is the chief pillar of the so-called Orthodox church, and it is often asserted, "convince the women of the superiority of the evangelical faith, and the men can be easily won." The older men and women do not appreciate the value of an education, but with the younger it is different, and the desire for improvement is strong. This is specially true at Perlepe, where one of the missionaries labors almost every Sabbath. Audiences are good, and sometimes ten hours at a time have been spent in religious conversation. The questions proposed are such as show much thought. All over Macedonia, it is believed, the fields are white for the harvest. In places where the missionaries have never been the word of God has found its way and worked mightily in turning men's minds from the errors of centuries. Many are convinced of the truth, and some are ready to say, and do say, that it is only a question of time; that the Protestant faith is true and will prevail.

The work of establishing a Girls' Boarding School has made satisfactory progress. Land has been purchased, and permission to build secured from Constantinople. The request was explicit for a private and not a public school.

The Vali was interested in the proposal, and a favorable reply came promptly, although there had been much reason to apprehend difficulty in securing it. The walls of the building are now going up, and will be ready for use this autumn. For the use of the school last year a house was purchased which can be sold again for what it cost

The arrival of Miss Crawford was very opportune, and she was able to be of immediate service in the English part of the instruction. From the very beginning the smile of God and the good will of man have rested on this school in a remarkable mariner. Macedonia needs the prayers of all. The political condition is deplorable. Outside of Monastir and Salonica, fear of the government, fear of robbers, fear of being falsely accused, prevails everywhere. At the late annual meeting of the mission, held in June last, several of the Bulgarian pastors and preachers were admitted to a share in the deliberations as corresponding members. They took an active part in the exercises, and gave proof of good judgment, as well as of earnest devotion to the cause of Christ. It is believed that a wise step was thus taken, of the greatest importance to the future harmonious cooperation of missionaries and the native Christians, while the latter have been led as never before to realize their personal responsibility for the progress of the gospel among their countrymen.

1882

72nd Annual Report
City Hall, Portland, Maine
October 3–6, 1882

Pages 23–26

European Turkey Mission — The general outlook is far more hopeful than ever before. Though embracing a field under three different governments, the mission is still one in its aims and plans, and is comparatively little affected by political conditions.

Monastir — In Monastir services have been held in the Girl's School Room, with larger audiences, and four persons have been admitted to communion. The sale of books has increased, and indicates greater readiness to read the Bible and missionary publications.

The Girls' Boarding School occupied its new building in October last, and rejoices in improved facilities for the growing work it has to do. The scholars number fifty, bright and intelligent youth, eight of whom are boarders. The interest manifested in the study of the Bible is very encouraging, and a missionary society has been organized among the pupils....

1883

73rd Annual Report
Central Methodist Church, Detroit, Michigan
October 2–5, 1883

Pages 30–34

European Turkey Mission — Of the four stations in this mission, only three are engaged in general missionary labor. Constantinople is the seat of the publishing department of all the Turkish missions, and, as such, has a part in the work for European Turkey. The three remaining stations, Monastir, Philippopolis, and Samokov, are now, as a result of the Russo-Turkish war, each under a different form of government; the first being in the Turkish province of Macedonia, and the others, respectively, in the province of Eastern Roumelia and the principality of Bulgaria. The lines of political division somewhat affect the character and results of the work, making the condition of affairs in the various stations less uniform than in many other missions. The three governments, unlike in most respects, are all alike hostile to Protestant Christianity.

Monastir — Preaching and Sabbath-school services have been well attended throughout the year, but without marked results. Occasional visits for Sabbath services have been made to the villages adjoining Monastir, and a cordial welcome generally received. One hundred and eighty days have been spent by missionaries in touring among the out-stations and the country around and beyond them. Their reports of these journeys are full of encouragement. Mr. Jenney says: "One cannot travel over Macedonia without being surprised at the great change in the people as regards a knowledge of the truth. Hundreds, who two years ago were in great ignorance and under the control of superstitions, to-day ,see plainly the errors of their church, and some, I believe, are trying to do God's will." At Isteep, at Uskub, and indeed at almost all the places visited, the doors were thrown wide open, and the people fairly begged for teachers. This is not the result of long years of human labor, but of the silent influences of the Holy Spirit.

Sickness prevented Mr. Jenney from completing an extensive tour, which he had planned, and it is hoped that the new year will witness still more of this widespread preaching of the Word. At Strumnitsa, the Greek Bishop made complaint, and the military commander ordered the helper to procure a government permit to preach, or, failing of this, to leave the city. By the aid of British Consul-General Blunt, the permission was obtained, and the preaching still goes on. At Uskub, also, there has been persecution, and the preacher has left this place to engage in evangelistic work among his own countrymen. Recently, as the colporter of this station was starting on a tour with a fresh supply of books, the official order came from Constantinople, requiring that all books offered for sale should be stamped by the government. A long delay was thereby occasioned, but the command must be obeyed. Such interference is trying to faith and patience;

but, with the signs of promise appearing in all directions, the laborers in this district thank God, and take courage.

Samokov — The report from this station is a song of thanksgiving for a deep and powerful work of the Spirit, which, beginning in the city itself during the winter, extended through the neighboring villages, and beyond the out-stations into Macedonia and Roumelia. Never before had there been seen such a thorough awakening of the people. ...

Education — The Girls' Boarding-School at Monastir has had an attendance of fourteen boarders and twenty day-scholars. most of whom have made good progress in their studies. The difference in nationality of the girls increases the difficulty of uniform instruction, and may necessitate the adoption of English as the school language. A case of discipline which threatened the peace of the whole church was, after long and careful treatment, satisfactorily settled.

1884
74th Annual Report
Second Presbyterian Church, Columbus, Ohio
October 7–10, 1884

Pages 24–25
Monastir — Preaching and Sabbath-school work have been sustained regularly in Monastir by the missionaries,

and in two out-stations by native preachers. The average attendance on worship in Monastir was sixty-five. A beginning has thus been made. Large sums from abroad, amounting to many thousands of dollars, have been spent on Greek, Bulgarian, and Romanian schools, with the intent of retaining a hold on the youth, and keeping them from attending mission schools; yet the girls' school of the mission has attracted over forty-three pupils, of whom thirty are day scholars. The importance of Monastir as a centre of influence is fully appreciated by others as well as ourselves.

1885

75th Annual Report
Tremont Temple, Boston, Massachusetts
October 13–16, 1885

Pages 25–28

European Turkey Mission — The year has been one of changes in this mission. ... Mr. and Mrs. Baird are enjoying a well-earned furlough, by a visit to this country, but return early this autumn. Their place has been supplied at Monastir by the removal of Mr. and Mrs. Locke from Samokov to Monastir.

The Bulgarian Evangelical Society continues its labors independently but in full accord with the mission, and assisted by grants-in-aid. Its principal care the past year has been devoted to the promising field in and about Sophia, the capital of the principality. A church of twenty members was organized in that city. Three preachers and a colporter have been employed by the society during the year, and also theological students from Samokov in the vacation of the Theological Institute. The society has also had part in the publication of several volumes much needed by the people.

The unsettled state of some portions of this mission field, especially in the region of which Monastir is the centre, has stood in the way of missionary effort, made touring dangerous, and greatly disturbed the minds of the people. Persecution of the bitterest kind has been experienced, in which Greek ecclesiastics have connived with the local authorities in the arrest and imprisonment of Protestants or of any who showed sympathy for them, under pretence of intrigues with brigands. The fidelity of the sufferers to their convictions has been a credit to the Christian name. Add to this the large sums spent by the old communities for education, and every effort to entice children and youth from mission schools, and it is obvious that progress, though slow, may well be regarded as sure and on substantial foundations. ...

Monastir — There is much to encourage in the hopeful spiritual condition of believers in this city. Eleven persons were received to communion during the year, two of them from the Girls' School. Mrs. Bond's medical work continues with a good degree of success. On days specially devoted to patients, sometimes as many as forty come to her for treatment. Besides this service for outsiders, her care for the girls in the boarding school is worthy of notice. This school, by the illness of Miss Spooner, was left to the charge of Miss Cole, while as yet but imperfectly in command of the language. But for the aid of Mr. and Mrs. Bond, it would have been quite impossible for her to have kept it up. The number of pupils enrolled during the year was forty-one—four Americans, four Albanians, three Greeks, three Gypsies, two Wallachians, and twenty-five Bulgarians. Of these, thirteen were boarders and twenty-eight day-scholars from the city.

The work is steadily progressing at the out-stations of Monastir, especially at Strumnitza and Monospetovo, though meeting most unjust and bitter persecution.

1886
76th Annual Report
Opera House, Des Moines, Iowa
October 5–8, 1886

Pages 28–30

Monastir—In spite of all hindrances from war, brigandage, and persecution in the out-stations, this station reports a prosperous year; larger audiences to hear the truth, more additions to the churches on confession of faith, more effort on the part of the people to help themselves, and new places for work opening faster than they can be supplied with laborers.

Schools — The Girls' School at Samokov had 54 pupils during the year, of whom 32 were boarders. Besides these there were 28 scholars in a primary department. Notwithstanding many unfavorable influences, the school was kept up as usual. There was no marked religious interest till near the close of the year, when a great awakening occurred, affecting the entire school, and all who had not previously professed themselves followers of Christ expressed a desire to begin a new life. A like blessing was enjoyed by the Girls' School at Monastir. The number of scholars enrolled was 45, 15 of them boarders, and 30 day-scholars from the city. This school, after a time, has won for itself a good reputation in that portion of the country.

The mission may well rejoice in the success of its schools the past year, and anticipate, in due time, a body of faithful co-laborers as the result of the late religious interest. It would not be easy to forecast the value of this spiritual awakening in these three most important centres of influence in its bearing on the future of this people.

1887

77th Annual Report
City Hall, Springfield, Massachusetts
October 4–7, 1887

Page 65

Monastir — The unsettled condition of the country has largely interfered with touring in this station, yet the work has become so well established at various out-stations that occasional visits have been sufficient to encourage the native brethren and secure a steady progress at most points. Many other agencies of value should be noted: Mrs. Baird's organization of a bi-weekly missionary society for girls; Mrs. Bond's bi-weekly lectures on various subjects calculated to interest and instruct boys of different nationalities, who swarm the streets in the neighborhood of missionary homes. Mrs. Bond's medical work continues to occupy a considerable portion of her time, and to enlarge her influence.

The Girls' Boarding School greatly needs an associate for Miss Cole. The school, however, has been well managed, though the number of girls has not been large. Of this station Mr. Bond reports that Protestantism is winning respect. "We are on excellent terms with the authorities in nearly every place." Thus the way is steadily opening for missionary effort in this portion of the field.

1888

78th Annual Report
Music Hall, Cleveland, Ohio
October 2–5, 1888

Pages 25–26

European Turkey Mission — The past year has been one of blessing to this mission. While the princes of this world have been prevented by mutual jealousies from any serious interference in the domestic affairs of the country, the gospel of Christ has had free course and been glorified. Never before have so many additions been made to the native churches; never before so widespread an interest in the truth, and so much to encourage vigorous effort to secure the evangelization of a most interesting people. New church edifices have been erected or enlarged, often wholly at the expense of the people themselves; and a larger number of pupils are seeking instruction in the girls' seminaries and in the Collegiate and Theological Institute for young men. With hardly an exception, the same report for substance is received from all parts of the field: larger congregations, more generous devotion to the work of Christ by pastors and Bible-women, not without striking examples of heroic endurance under trial and self-sacrifice for the truth.

1889

79th Annual Report
Tabernacle Congregational Church, New York City
October 15–18, 1889

Page 36

European Turkey Mission — In the neighborhood of Monastir an interesting work seems ready to open among the Albanians, and Mr. Baird is eager to begin labor among them by means of some of their young men who are in attendance upon our schools.

1890

80th Annual Report
Plymouth Congregational Church, Minneapolis, Minnesota
October 8–11, 1890

Pages 32–34

European Turkey Mission — At the recent annual meeting of the European Turkey Mission held at Monastir, the prevailing sentiment was one of hope and encouragement for the future ... Churches have not yet been organized in connection with Monastir station, for want of suitable pastors. It is hoped that this want will be supplied from young men now in training at Samokov. Pastoral care has hitherto devolved on the missionaries, and has been limited to such attention as they could give while touring. ...

Special interest is felt by the mission in the opening of Albania, a region bordering upon Monastir station. Through the agency of the British and Foreign Bible Society, many copies of the Scriptures have found their way among the people, and some of their youth have obtained an education at our higher schools. A native Albanian of promise, after completing his education has now been ordained to carry the gospel to his countrymen. As expressive of the interest among these people, an old man in one place offers to bear all the expenses of a school, if the mission will open it. Another pledges the use of his house for a school and the support of two teachers. Another has purchased two hundred copies, and another thirty copies, of a portion of the Scriptures, Genesis and Matthew, for distribution. In view of the interest awakened among this people, Mr. Baird, of Monastir, has decided to devote some portion of his time to the study of the Albanian language. Mr. Kyrias, just ordained to the gospel ministry, will heartily cooperate with Mr. Baird. The movement has begun with so much promise and at comparatively so small expense that it is hoped it may be continued in the same spirit and that the missionary enterprise among this people may be largely independent of foreign aid. ...

The work ... of this station [Monastir] as a whole, especially with its outlook into Albania and the successful girls' school, is one of great promise for the future.

1891

81st Annual Report
First Congregational Church, Pittsfield, Massachusetts
October 13–16, 1891

Pages 27–28

European Turkey Mission — Allusion has been made on several occasions to the work begun among the Albanians. The illness of Mr. Baird for several months has prevented pushing that work as rapidly as was anticipated, but a genuine interest in the gospel has been developed, and it is hoped that a beginning has been made for the establishment of Christian institutions among this interesting people.

1892

82nd Annual Report
First Congregational Church, Chicago, Illinois
October 4–7, 1892

Pages 30–31

European Turkey Mission — The general work of the mission has been carried on substantially as heretofore. The educational work has had a prominent place in the thought of the mission through the collegiate and theological institutes at Samokov and the two high schools for girls, one at Samokov and one at Monastir. The number of students in attendance at these institutions has been about the same as in former years, with the exception of

Monastir, where the attendance was somewhat larger. Efforts are constantly making to raise the standard of education in these institutions, and at the same time to maintain a thoroughly efficient Christian influence that may tell on the religious character and life of the pupils. A good deal of personal interest in religion has been manifested among these pupils, especially in the girls' schools.

The evangelistic work has been well sustained by personal labors of missionaries, preaching as they have had opportunity at their various stations and engaging in tours quite generally among the churches, where their presence has been found most valuable for counsel and for the encouragement of native preachers. Indeed no part of missionary work is of more value than that of touring by the missionaries, especially when accompanied by their wives. It is difficult to overestimate the influence which a missionary and his wife may exert by a visit of a few days in one of the native Christian communities. The suggestions they are able to give the native teachers and preachers are of the greatest value, not only as instruction, but as encouragement to these faithful laborers, often overburdened with care and anxiety, and sometimes subjected to bitter opposition on the part of the enemies of the truth. ...

In addition to the work for the Bulgarians an interesting beginning has been made among the Albanians through young men and young women from Albania, who had found their way to our schools and there embraced the gospel. One family especially has done admirable service for their countrymen in teaching, as well as in preaching the gospel.

The Albanians occupy a high, mountainous region between Macedonia and the Adriatic, formerly known as Epirus and Illyricum, embracing a population variously estimated from 750,000 to 1,200,000. Their language is one of the most complicated, and bears traces of the fusion of the various languages spoken by the different races and peoples that have been driven into these mountain fastnesses by their neighbors—from the Pelasgic, Greek, Turkish, and a variety of Sclavic stocks. These people have long been known as furnishing the bravest soldiery in the Turkish armies and are characterized by native vigor and energy quite equal to that possessed by any other race in Europe. The interest already shown by a few in the gospel of Christ and their readiness to contribute to its promulgation are indicative of a better future for these brave mountaineers.

1893

83rd Annual Report
Mechanics Hall, Worchester, Massachusetts
October 10–13, 1893

Page 30
European Turkey Mission — Mr. Baird, besides his proper work in the Monastir station, is improving every opportunity to introduce the gospel among the Albanians,

a people hitherto unreached. An interesting beginning has been made through Albanian students educated at our schools.

1894

84th Annual Report
First Congregational Church, Madison, Wisconsin
October 10, 1894

Pages 29–30

Samokov —Special interest is felt in the Collegiate and Theological Institute by the members of the mission as the only means of furnishing suitable men for pushing forward the evangelistic work. The loss by death of several devoted laborers within the past two or three years, as Mr. Boyadjieff, late of Sophia, and more recently Mr. Kyrias, who had entered upon the Albanian work with so much of hope and promise, has led the mission to feel as never before the value of this Institute if suitable men are to be raised up to aid the missionaries in the general work of evangelization.

Monastir — The younger Mr. Haskell, after some delays in crossing the border from Bulgaria into Macedonia, has found abundant opportunity of work in connection with Mr. Baird, at Monastir. These brethren have done a good deal of most valuable touring work in different parts of the field and have supplied, as well as they could, the place of pastors and native preachers by occasional visits to different points. Their work has been greatly hindered for want of men to second them in their efforts, and the lack of pastors and preachers. They find a degree of interest at many points which greatly encourages them, and they are confident that, could work be properly followed up, much might be accomplished at an early da y in Macedonia. Much of the time and strength of Mr. Baird have been given to the work in Albania, which was begun a few years since through native Albanians trained in our schools. The death of Mr. Kyrias, the most promising one of these helpers, has thrown the work back; still it is felt that a good beginning has been made.

The Girls' School at Monastir has been well sustained by Miss Cole in the absence of her associate in America, aided by Miss Baird, the daughter of the missionary. The number of pupils is not large, but the importance of the school in raising up young women to be teachers in the various villages and cities from which they come cannot be overestimated.

1895

85th Annual Report
Academy of Music, Brooklyn, New York
October 15–18, 1895

Pages 35–37

European Turkey Mission — The most important change in this mission is the establishing of a new station in Salonica. The missionaries, Rev. J. H. House and Rev. E. B. Haskell, have been transferred thither with their families, and nineteen out-stations have been passed into their care. Salonica is regarded as the most commanding centre for the Macedonian field and has the advantage of good railway communication with outlying towns. ...

Monastir — The most productive portions of this field have been passed over to the new Salonica station, as contemplated last year. The remaining district, which includes nine out-stations, has been faithfully worked, under various discouragements, by two missionaries, their wives, and native helpers. The church in Monastir became divided over a matter of no great consequence, but the disaffected party withdrew and held separate services. In January, upon invitation, Mr. Bond became their pastor, but not until the people had given some evidence of union. ...

The Albanian work is hopeful. The girls' day-school, the only girls' school using the Albanian language, has been excellently managed by native teachers. Its closing exercises attracted a large number of the best citizens of

Kortcha. Several books are now ready to be printed for this people. The government has finally given permission for the whole Bible to be printed in Albanian.

Salonica — A great need is felt for funds for evangelists, Bible-women, and one colporter. The workers have special solicitude concerning the education of Macedonian evangelical boys, for whom there is no school nearer than Samokov. It is greatly desired that permission for such a school as is needed may be granted by the government. ...

1896
86th Annual Report
First Congregational Church, Toledo, Ohio
October 6–9, 1896

Page 36

Monastir — We now pass into the Turkish side of the European Turkey Mission. It must be borne in mind that a large part of this station was given to Salonica when the division was made two years ago and Salonica was opened as a new station. The work outside of Monastir is in its infancy, and the people are poor and are growing poorer. The station has been able to secure and employ but few native helpers. There are many places where work should be attempted.

The Girls' Boarding School has had during the year twenty-four pupils in attendance in the main school, of whom three were boys, and thirteen in the kindergarten, of whom four were boys, making in all thirty-seven. Of these, thirteen were boarders. The boarders were from seven places in the field.

1897

87th Annual Report
Hyperion Opera House, New Haven, Connecticut
October 12–15, 1897

Pages 36–40

European Turkey Mission — Of the five stations of this mission, three are in Turkey and two in Bulgaria. The three stations in Turkey have been subject to all the uncertainty, hardship, and danger of riots, massacre, and war. Constantinople, which is the headquarters for the publication work of the mission, has been in a chronic state of uncertainty and disturbance during the year, and after war was declared between Turkey and Greece in the spring, Salonica was an important military post upon the Turkish side, and Monastir occupied an uncertain position between the Bulgarians, the Albanians, the Greeks, and the Turks, in case the troubles should extend to the north. During all the trouble the missionaries remained at their stations and none of them were disturbed. The Turkish soldiers and officials have been very orderly in all their movements, few acts of depredation being charged to them by the missionaries. ...

In the Collegiate and Theological Institute at Samokov the number of students enrolled has been fifty, of whom four have left. There was no fifth or sixth class last year, and hence this year the six and seventh classes are wanting. The four students in last year's seventh, or Theological Class, are all at work as preachers of the gospel, and seem to be useful laborers. The influence of the school is not confined to Bulgaria and Macedonia, as one of the above four is at work in Albania among his own people. This school has close relations to the evangelization of Bulgaria. It is of the utmost importance that it be better sustained financially. It can never do the work necessary in the preparation of a native ministry until it is endowed to some extent, so as to allow it to lay out a more liberal course of study and furnish a better training for its students.

Monastir — During the greater part of the year under review Mr. Baird was in Bitlis, Eastern Turkey, aiding Mr. Cole, who was left there alone. Owing to the absence of Mr. Baird and the unsettled condition of the country, Mr. Bond and the ladies have been able to do but little touring. ... Amid all the political agitations of the year the city was never more peaceful. Thousands of soldiers passed through the city for the front, but were exceedingly orderly, almost without exception.

The Girls' Boarding School has been under the efficient care of Miss Cole and Miss Matthews. During the year twenty-four pupils have been in attendance in the main school and ten in the primary department.

1898

88th Annual Report
Park Congregational Church, Grand Rapids, Michigan
October 4–7, 1898

Pages 37, 40

European Turkey Mission, Samokov — This is the largest station of the mission. It has, at the center, in the city of Samokov, the Collegiate and Theological Institute and the Boarding School for Girls. The population of the field is 350,000 souls. During the year work has been carried on in eight places outside the city. There are three ordained native pastors; two of them are teaching in the city. There are five unordained preachers connected with the station, making a total of twenty native assistants, including male and female teachers. The people paid for the support of their own institutions nearly nine hundred dollars. There were 125 pupils under the instruction of the mission; all of them are in Samokov, as all of the children in the outstations are in attendance upon the national schools. The evangelistic work in the field has continued with little to give it distinctive character. ...

Monastir has only three outstations, with a total of eleven native helpers. Its field, however, includes 1,300,000 souls. This statement shows how inadequately the field is worked. Mr. Bond has been without an associate in the general work.

The Girls' Boarding School has had a prosperous year. In her report from the school Miss Matthews[2] says:

> When school opened in September, fifteen boarders were present. Before the middle of the fall term, the house was full. Every available place was occupied, excepting a small room reserved for sickness. For each of the twenty-one boarders, three, and in five cases, four, liras (one lira equals $4.40) have been received. The proportion of little girls is larger than usual, and caused more or less difficulty in arranging the domestic work. In the winter it became necessary to have a matron, and the services of a Protestant woman were secured. Her only daughter lives with her, and attends school, making twenty-two pupils in the house. Eight pupils from the city have been enrolled, making a total of thirty.
>
> In accordance with the expression of the mission at its last meeting, the study of English has been advanced as much as possible, with a view to making it the language of the school, thus opening up the privileges of the institution to girls of other races, especially those of Albania. With this object, Miss Matthews has given considerable time to the study of Albanian. There are three resident Bulgarian teachers, all graduates of this school, and one of them a graduate of the Samokov school, also. An excellent spirit has prevailed among teachers and scholars. The religious life of the school has been steady and earnest. As always, we believe that the required time for prayer and Bible reading every morning and evening is one of the most potent influences for good. The School C. E. Society has

---

2 Miss Mary L. Matthews (1864–1950) served in Monastir in 1888–1920.

been well sustained. Nearly every girl belongs to it. It was organized in 1892 as a Junior Society, but as the girls grew older it was changed to a Y. P. S. C. E. There are at present twelve active and twelve associate members. All the officers are pupils. It is our earnest desire to have more of the best girls in training to become helpers in the work, which, if done at all, must be done by them, for the uplifting and salvation of woman in this land.

1899

89th Annual Report
Union Congregational Church, Providence, Rhode Island
October 3–6, 1899

Pages 41–49

European Turkey Mission, Historical Notes — In 1858 explorations were made in Bulgaria with a view to opening mission work there. Two years before this date the American Methodist Church (North) had sent missionaries to the Bulgarian territory north of the Balkan, where they have carried on a work to the present time. Drs. Hamlin and Elias Riggs made extended tours of investigation in preparation for the opening of the mission. In 1840, under the care of the British and Foreign Bible Society, a translation of the New Testament was made into Bulgarian. Owing to inaccuracies in translation and great changes in the spoken language itself, Dr. Riggs of our mission, aided by Dr. A. L. Long of the Methodist Episcopal Mission and two Bulgarian scholars, revised the

New Testament and translated the Old, and the entire Bulgarian Bible was issued at Constantinople in 1864. The following year the New Testament was issued by the same translators in another Bulgarian dialect, and in 1874 a new revised edition of the entire Bible, made by Dr. Riggs, was published. This Bible work and exploration was preparatory to the opening of the mission of our Board in 1871. At that time Constantinople was made the center for the work of publication in the Bulgarian language. In 1870, the year previous to the formal opening of the Bulgarian or European Turkey Mission, the press at Constantinople issued over 5,000,000 pages of Christian literature in the Bulgarian language. The *Zornitza* ("Morning Star"), originally issued as a monthly but changed later to a weekly, has been published since the formation of the mission. It was temporarily suspended in 1897 on account of lack of funds. ...

Our mission work is directed almost exclusively to the Bulgarians, although Turks, Greeks, Albanians and some other races are within the field. The legitimate mission field, for which no other Board is at work, comprises fully four and a quarter million souls. ...

Monastir — This station was divided in 1894, Salonica taking the most of the outstations, only three remaining with the mother station. The unoccupied field of the station, however, embraces no less than 1,300,000 souls. For its care there is only one ordained American missionary, Mr. Bond and his wife, and two single ladies for the school, assisted by ten trained Bulgarians. Within the limits of this field are that interesting people, the Albanians, who seem eager for Christian enlightenment. The one church in connection with this station added to its membership last year fourteen on confession of faith. A male Christian Endeavor Society was organized in January. Hitherto some of the Christians had an antipathy to a binding pledge. A year ago a large Boys' Bulgarian Boarding School was opened on premises adjoining our Girls' Boarding School. This school was recently broken up because one of the favorite teachers was summarily dismissed by the bishop for giving utterance in public to his belief that the Scriptures should be read in the churches in a language which the people could understand. The students in a body withdrew with the teacher. At Kortcha, the work among the Wallachians is encouraging. When Mr. Bond was there the audiences numbered from 80 to 150. The pastor, Mr. Sinas, has devoted some of his time during the year to translating portions of the Albanian Scriptures from the Greek lettering to the new Albanian alphabet. There were fifty girls in our school at this place, but during the winter a double order came from Constantinople, compelling the withdrawal of all Mohammedan girls. The fathers were exceedingly pleased with the school. One of their leaders, a Bey, offered the free use of a room in his house for a school if the mission would furnish a Christian teacher. This is the only girls' school in the country in which Albanian is used, and the only Albanian school for boys is in Kortcha. The governor of the province is an Albanian, who is favorable to the missionaries and their work. The two colporters have spent an aggregate of 454 days in the field, and their sales have amounted to nearly 1,400 piastres. The report of the general station work closes with the statement that "evangelical Christianity is steadily gaining ground in the station, and that there are many genuine protestants in the field who are not numbered in the statistics."

Girls' Boarding School [Monastir] — This school has continued under the joint principalship of the Misses Cole and Matthews. The pupils have numbered twenty-four, fourteen of whom were boarders. Twelve of these were Bulgarians, five Servians, three Albanians, three Wallachians, and one a Jew. Owing to the large number of nationalities represented, English has been made the language of the school. ...

In November, 1898, the first General Conference of the Protestant churches and communities in Macedonia was held in the village of Murtino, to recognize the new church then organized and to consider questions pertaining to the general progress of Christian work. The policeman sent by the Turkish government to watch the proceeding was so impressed by the large and enthusiastic gathering that he afterwards defended the protestants in the presence of other officials.

The work done by Miss Stone from this center is of profound interest. She has general charge of the evangelistic work for women in the entire mission. If she is not a bishop, certainly her labors almost entitle her to the name. Since her return to the mission last October, she has spent almost half of her time in touring over the field, arousing the women, and organizing the work. Her first call is for more native helpers to take possession and hold the places already won for Christ. The possibilities of her field are limitless.

1900

90th Annual Report
Pilgrim Congregational Church, St. Louis, Missouri
October 10–12, 1900

Pages 41–42

Monastir — This station covers a large but as yet uncultivated territory, including many of that interesting race, the Albanians. The population of the field of this station is estimated at more than one and a quarter million. The station and mission are eager to begin direct Christian work for the Albanians, some of whom have already shown themselves to be earnest Christians. Many who have not professed their belief in Christ are eager for Christian schools and are ready to help support Christian institutions. There are only three outstations, with a total of nine native assistants, including the teachers in the school at Monastir.

Mr. and Mrs. Bond have done considerable touring over the field of this station, finding in many places encouragement and cheer. The Protestants of Monastir are endeavoring to secure recognition as a separate community according to the custom in many parts of Turkey.

Mr. Sinas, the Albanian preacher at Kortcha, was absent from his post by permission nearly four months, engaged at Constantinople in the translation of the New Testament and Psalms from the Greek lettering to the new and popular Albanian alphabet. The Sunday services are well attended by a hopeful class of young people. Aside from evangelical work, Mr. Sinas teaches in the Girls' School. The attendance at the school has gone up to over forty, many having been turned away for lack of accommodation.

Miss Kyrias writes of the joy of the teachers in their work; praises the excellent behavior of the girls and notes their interest in Bible study. Mohammedan parents are still forbidden to send their daughters, but a number of them quietly gather in the harem of one of the beys and are taught by a graduate of the school — a Christian. An attempt has been made to assassinate the governor because of his friendliness for the Christian population.

The Girls' Boarding School [in Monastir] has had twenty-two boarders and fourteen day scholars, the largest number in the history of the school. Five nationalities are represented: Bulgarian, Albanian, Servian, Roumanian and Austrian. English is the language of the school and all branches of mathematics have been taught in it. Failures, in certain cases, to make the required progress, seem due to lack of ability, rather than the change of language. The fourth class, consisting of one Bulgarian, one Albanian, and one Servian, has been taking Bible study, Geometry, Physics, Literature and History in English, satisfactorily. The pupils are graded as follows: fourth class, three; advanced second class, three; second class, three; first class, five; preparatory, nine; and primary, ten. Several of the pupils became Christians during the year. The school needs larger accommodations in order to take all who apply for admission. ...

1901

91st Annual Report
Parsons Opera House, Hartford, Connecticut
October 8–11, 1901

Pages 41–43

Monastir —In Monastir the missionary force consists of one missionary family and two single ladies. The work is both educational and evangelistic, and the native workers are four ordained preachers and six teachers. The work is for Bulgarians and Albanians. That for the Bulgarians centers in Monastir, and that for the Albanians in Kortcha. There is one organized church, which is Bulgarian, with sixty-nine communicants. The contributions of the people for their own work were $510.75.

The evangelical work in this district seems to meet with more difficulties than in any other station. In the cities there are many ready to listen to the gospel message, but there is need of the moving power of the Spirit to bring them to the decision to take up their cross and suffer for Christ and his Kingdom. The missionary and his wife have done much touring together, and find many listeners and apparent sympathizers with the truth, and are encouraged to feel that their labors are not in vain in the Lord. This preparatory work must be carried on, and the seed sown with patience.

The Girls' Boarding School in Monastir reports a total enrollment of thirty-seven, of whom seventeen were boarders. This is the largest number of boarders they have ever had from outside of the city. This school has furnished many good Bible workers for the Salonica station. The visiting trustee reports the discipline and morale of the school as excellent. The work done in the class rooms was also much commended.

The Albanian Girls' Boarding School in Kortcha has also had a prosperous year. The teachers in this school are all natives. Miss Kyrias is much commended by the missionaries of Monastir and Salonica, who have visited the school, for the ability with which she has conducted this institution. This is the first year that boarders have been received. Their number was five. At the closing exercises a large audience was present, including several Albanian beys, among whom was the governor of the city, who made an address commending the work of the school.

The arrest of Mr. Sinas, the Albanian preacher at Berat, his release upon bail, but his virtual exile from that place and from his family, who are in Kortcha, has necessitated an appeal for aid to our legation at Constantinople. It is hoped that he soon may be able to return to his work. ...

The political disturbances in Macedonia have been of the most serious character during the year, and the prisons have been filled with those who have been implicated, or suspected of being implicated, in the insurrectionary movement. What with insurrection, bad harvests, and the consequent financial stringency, the condition of the province has been most distressing. It was feared at one time that little missionary work could be done. Illness among the missionaries also greatly complicated the situation. Notwithstanding all these difficulties, the work has gone on with unexpected interest. The dark clouds that have overshadowed the land seem to have turned some hearts towards God, the refuge of troubled souls. Unexpected seriousness and religious interest has been found in some towns and villages, e.g., Doiran, Upper and Lower Todorak, Eleshnitza, and Goleshovo. Some 287 days of touring have been put in by the different members of the station, in spite of difficulties. The need of more ordained workers is most urgent, but it seems difficult to find the men, to say nothing of the means.

The Servian work in Prishtina, and Mitrovitza, and surrounding town, is an interesting and growing work. The first Servian school of the mission has finished a successful year in Prishtina. On the whole, this has been a year of progress and blessing.

1902

92nd Annual Report
First Congregational Church, Oberlin, Ohio
October 14–17, 1902

Pages 40–46

European Turkey Mission — The one event in the mission that has absorbed attention, weighed upon the hearts of the missionaries, and demanded time and strength, was the capture, in Macedonia, of Miss Ellen M. Stone and Madame Katharina S. Tsilka by Macedonian brigands on the 3d of September, 1901, and their retention in captivity until the 23d of February, 1902 — one hundred and seventy-two (172) days.

In August, Miss Stone had conducted in Bansko, Macedonia, in the Raslog district, a summer training class for the Bulgarian teachers in the mission primary schools and for the Bible-women who are working in connection with the Salonica station. The school closed, and a party numbering thirteen persons, all natives of the country except Miss Stone, conducted by a caravan of seven men, set out upon their return journey towards Salonica. On the main road, between Bansko and Djuma, within a short distance from a Turkish guard house, on September 3d, they were attacked by a large party of brigands, and the entire party captured. A little later all were released except Miss Stone and Madame Tsilka. These were swiftly taken into the fastnesses of the mountains and kept in concealment.

On the day of the capture the event was reported far and wide, and unusual interest was aroused in the fate of these two women, alone in the hands of brigands, who have long been known for their severity to captives. On September 24th, a message was received at Samokov from the captors, stating that the brigands demanded a ransom of 25,000£ T, or $110,000. It was announced at the same time that unless this sum was raised and paid over in twenty days, the lives of the captives would be in jeopardy. The American Board could not establish the dangerous precedent of ransoming one of its missionaries, but in view of the recommendation of President Roosevelt and the Secretary of State, about two-thirds of this sum was quickly raised by popular subscription and put into the hands of the United States Government, to negotiate terms with the captors, pay the ransom, and receive the prisoners.

Subsequently, long delays ensued, and for many weeks rumors were rife that the captives had both been slain. In January communications were again opened with the brigands, which gave assurance that both the captives were alive and well. President Roosevelt and the entire State Department interested themselves in the case, and Minister Leishman, at Constantinople, and Consul Dickinson, the Diplomatic Agent to Bulgaria, were directed to employ every legitimate agency to secure information of the captives and to effect their release. Attempts to negotiate from Sofia, the capital of Bulgaria, failed. Finally, Mr. Gargiulo, First Dragoman of the United States Legation at Constantinople, W. W. Peet, Esq., the Treasurer of the Turkish Missions, and Rev. J. Henry House, d.d., a member of the European Turkey Mission, began operations in Salonica and proceeded northwards to Macedonia, until they got in communication, with representatives of the brigand band, and after having come to terms, paid over to them 15,500£ T, or $68,200 in gold. The captives were to be delivered later.

Owing to the unusual activity of Turkish troops, the prisoners were not delivered as agreed, but some three weeks after the ransom was paid, on the morning of the 23d of February, they were left to wander alone, with the little girl babe born to Madam Tsilka in her captivity, into the town of Strumnitsa, in Macedonia, where they were among friends once more.

Contrary to every anticipation, the released captives were in good health and spirits — although their imprisonment had been full of peril and hardships. They were soon met by their missionary associates from Salonica, to which place they returned. After a few weeks' quiet there, Miss Stone came to America for much needed rest, and since her arrival in this country, on the 10th of April, has been much in demand to tell the story of her capture, imprisonment, and release.

During the time of the captivity, from September 3[3] to February 23, the entire mission force bore a heavy burden of anxiety. No effort was spared to learn of the

---

3 The original was printed December 3, in error. A handwritten note in the original manuscript corrects this to September 3.

whereabouts of the band and the condition of the captives. Even the routine work of the mission suffered. At the same time there was much political unrest, both upon the Bulgarian and upon the Turkish side of the line. The native Christians in Macedonia suffered greatly from the lawless acts of wandering bands of brigands, who carried on their profession with little or no restraint. Under conditions like these has the work of the year been prosecuted. The missionaries have been compelled to, exercise great caution in the prosecution of their outside touring and evangelistic work, not to expose themselves to capture by the various brigand bands that roved over the mountains of Macedonia.

There are four stations in this mission: two (Philippopolis and Samokov) in Bulgaria and two (Monastir and Salonica) are in Macedonia, and so are within Turkish territory and subject to Turkish rule. Miss Clarke resides at Sofia, the capital of Bulgaria, where there is a large Protestant church and community, but this is not accounted as a station of the mission. ...

The school at Kortcha has had from six to eight boarders, with fifty on the rolls. ...

Monastir — The work for the Albanians centers in Kortcha, and the principal worker is Mr. Tsilka, the husband of Mrs. Tsilka, who was the companion of Miss Stone in her captivity. The school at Kortcha reports forty-five pupils, of whom eight are boarders. It has been impossible for the missionaries at this station to do much touring, on account of the unsafe condition of the country. It seemed best for personal as well as international reasons not to take unnecessary risks.

The report of the Girls' School at Monastir has not been received. Dr. House, in closing his report, says:

> On the whole, the year has been one of great difficulty in the evangelical work in Macedonia on account of the widespread influence of the revolutionary movement throughout the province, and one of great sorrow and heavy burdens on account of the abduction of Miss Stone and her companion, Mrs. Tsilka. In spite of all, however, we have had many blessings and much to encourage us to think that we may soon see spiritual awakenings in many portions of our field.

1903
93rd Annual Report
First Congregational Church, Manchester, New Hampshire
October 13–16, 1903

Pages 39, 43

European Turkey Mission — The political disturbance in the Macedonian part of the mission, including the two stations of Monastir and Salonica, has been increasingly annoying if not alarming during the year. Mrs. Haskell's death occurred only a few days after severe disturbance in Salonica, when the Ottoman Bank was blown up almost under the walls of the mission house. There was no little bloodshed in the city at that time. In and about Monastir there has been even a more alarming uprising. Insurgents from Bulgaria and armed bands from Macedonia have attacked Turkish soldiers, who in turn have preyed upon the Christian population. This state of affairs has rendered the conditions abnormal and made the work difficult all of the time and perilous, if not impossible, some of the time. The missionaries have remained at their posts, continuing the various departments of their work, not thinking it wise to make any changes in view of the disturbed state of the country. Their presence has enabled them to alleviate suffering and to comfort the distracted. They have felt it to be their duty and privilege to remain among the people to whom they have devoted their lives, and share with them their sorrows. It has been possible to do but little touring in Macedonia, although in the earlier part of the year many outstations were visited. In Bulgaria the political situation has not been so alarming, although the sympathies of the Bulgarians throughout the country have been strong with their struggling people over the line in Turkish territory. This has made it impossible for the students as well as others to settle down to sober and quiet work.

The following detailed report, however, shows that during the year good progress has been made, and there is every reason to feel encouraged. The missionaries have maintained a neutral attitude, not taking part in the political agitations either in Macedonia or in Bulgaria. Their mission to those countries is not a political one, and as such they are recognized by all classes.

Monastir — Monastir is ninety miles northwest of Salonica and includes Albania. In his report Mr. Bond says:

> Considering the political situation in the Monastir field we have reason enough to praise God for what has been accomplished. Many of the newspaper reports have been exaggerated. During the year we have been kept at this station in comparative quiet, the chief excitement consisting in wholesale arrests, an occasional assassination, and reports of bloody encounters in neighboring villages.

Work at the station has been well sustained. Three new members have been added to the church; the preaching services have been well attended, and the young people flock to the Sunday school. At Kortcha Mr. Tsilka has been much encouraged. The girls' school there, with fifty-three pupils, which is the only school in which the Albanian language is used, has had a prosperous year. At the closing exercises of the school the Albanian governor, who is brother-in-law to the grand vizier at Constantinople, was present, occupying the seat of honor. The girls' boarding school at Monastir has enlarged its capacity to meet the increasing number of pupils. Forty-six have been in attendance, of whom twenty were boarders. The school work has been but little disturbed during the year.

Salonica — Salonica, a seaport, is the leading city of Macedonia. The year since the last report has been, in many respects, the most trying in the history of the station.

The lawlessness and anarchy prevailing throughout much of the field has restricted touring largely to the railway lines. But for the unsettled condition of the country two men would have been ordained and a separate church organized. The feeling that it was not best to gather people for councils has prevented this. ... The Albanians in that part of the country seem especially well disposed towards our work.

1904
94th Annual Report
First Congregational Church, Grinnell, Iowa
October 11–13, 1904

Pages 37–38, 43

European Turkey Mission — Since the last report was issued Mr. Thomson has resumed work in Samokov, leaving Mrs. Thomson in Scotland, who was obliged to remain behind for health reasons beyond the furlough period. After thirty-six years of labor in the mission Mr. and Mrs. Bond find themselves compelled to withdraw from the work, and have come to America to establish a new home. Their leaving is a cause of deep regret to their fellow missionaries and colaborers, and the sorrow of their departure is shared by the Bulgarian workers. Miss Matthews has come to the States for her regular furlough. The Holways have been transferred to Monastir, as the return of Dr. and Mrs. House will reenforce the Salonica station, to provide for the vacancy left by the withdrawal of the Bonds.

The regular work of the European Turkey Mission has been no less disturbed in the year under review than for the last three years, and in some respects the disturbances have been more critical. In the early spring of last year insurgent bands entered Macedonia and were met there by large bodies of Turkish troops. More or less of a desultory conflict was carried on during the summer and into the autumn. Between the contending parties the villages suffered intensely; the Turkish villages from the depredations of the insurgents and the Christian villages from the Turkish troops. An appeal was made in the autumn for relief for those who were left without home and shelter, and entirely destitute of food, and with but little clothing. This appeal met a cordial response in both England and America, the Christian Herald of New York sending considerable sums for distribution during the winter. The missionaries of Salonica and Monastir, on either side of the Turkish line, gave themselves very fully to relief work, and in this work they were protected by Turkish officials. The missionaries in Bulgaria looked after refugees who fled over the line, for whose needs the Bulgarian government in large part provided. Mr. Bond at Monastir was made treasurer of the relief funds, and Monastir was the principal distributing station, as it is in the district of largest depredation.

It became necessary to provide for orphans in connection with the girls' school at Monastir, owing to the condition of a large number of children who were left unprotected. The missionaries at Salonica secured a piece of land, some sixty acres, and are making preparation to start an industrial work for boys to be connected with the school of intermediate grade. This plan has received the approval of the mission. Through the kindly offices of Miss Stone, the site is already partly paid for, and the station is planning to put up a building for the home. It has practically become a settled policy, not only of this mission, but of all the missions of the Board, not to provide homes for orphan children without at the same time affording them an opportunity to earn, in a measure at least, their own living while studying. Experience has proven that this develops a strength of character that can be developed in no other way, and in many instances it provides a trade which makes the child independent when he is able to go out and begin for himself.

The present prospect for political quiet is more encouraging than a year ago. While the Bulgarians and Christian Macedonians have little confidence in the promised reform, they have been in a measure exhausted by their struggle for liberty. There is therefore every reason to expect that in the year to come there will be less disturbance and more opportunity for direct, aggressive Christian work. As will be seen from the following reports, however, there has been much progress in the year under review.

Monastir — A large part of the time of the missionaries here has been given to the relief work, which compelled attention. The ordinary lines of missionary effort have been carried on, but less effectively in some departments. Not a single tour has been made by a missionary, which is accounted for by the unsettled condition of the country in the earlier months of the year, and -the claims of relief work in the latter half. For like reasons there was an almost complete failure of colportage. The church records show only two accessions during the year (one of these a boarder in the girls' school), but allowance should here be made for the absorption of mind and heart in distracting politics.

The special occasion for interest in the year was the commemoration in March of the centennial of the British and Foreign Bible Society. In the service, held in the mission chapel, four languages were used, Albanian, Bulgarian, Greek, and English, and many distinguished citizens were present.

Kortcha, the center for the Albanian work, has been without a pastor this year, as Mr. Tsilka remained in America. At a time when traveling was especially dangerous, in September, Miss Kyrias, in company with one of the other teachers, heroically returned to Kortcha; and in spite of determined opposition of the Greek bishop and his tools, the school was promptly opened, and was continued with a good degree of success, the attendance averaging thirty-three.

The American School for Girls [in Monastir] has continued its work without the expected interruption, with fifty-one pupils enrolled at the opening of the fall term, thirty-three of these in the boarding department. Five nationalities were represented. As previously stated, this school was obliged to provide for some orphans left destitute by the devastations of the Turks. The summer vacation proved a most trying time to the teachers who were obliged to remain in Monastir. The school has a Senior and Junior Endeavor Society.

1905
95th Annual Report
Plymouth Congregational Church, Seattle, Washington
September 14–18, 1905

Page xvi
I. The Primary Work of the Board — The conviction that the best way to serve humanity is first to persuade men to come into conscious fellowship with Christ has led the Board to put its primary emphasis upon evangelistic effort.

II. The Secondary Work of the Board — Not only because Christianity cares for the whole man, physical and mental as well as spiritual, has the Board established medical and educational work, but because, through its secondary agencies, it finds opportunity for fulfilling its chief mission....

This report is filled with facts which quicken the pulse and fill the eye with visions of the city whose maker and builder is God. From each of these missions comes some call.... In European Turkey the way is open for a work among the Albanians.

Pages 34–35, 38

European Turkey Mission — The school at Kortcha in Albania and for Albanians has been forbidden by the government to use the Albanian language. It is expected that after the school property has been transferred to the mission, which is now under consideration, as an American school it will be permitted to continue its Albanian teaching. The mission is unanimous in feeling that the time is fully ripe to open work for the Albanian people, and they call for a missionary to be appointed for this purpose. This hardy, able race seems to be accessible, and is even eager to have the mission begin regular work among them....

Monastir is in Macedonia and on the Turkish side of the line. The church has had no pastor during the year, the missionary, Mr. Clarke, serving as acting pastor. They are hoping soon to have a pastor of their own, and this will undoubtedly bring them new and greater force. An orphanage has been opened at Monastir through funds largely furnished by the Bible Lands Missions' Aid Society, in which some twenty girls and fourteen boys have found a home. These orphans are products of the troubles of 1903, and funds are in hand in the mission to conduct the orphan home for some time. Monastir has five outstations, but in a field which is at the present time unworked, and with a population of over one and a quarter million of souls. The Albanian region comes within the borders of the Monastir field. There has been no preacher for the Albanians at Kortcha, but the teacher in the school has had regular services for the pupils and a few others who have attended. In the absence of the regular teacher for the Albanian Girls' Boarding School at Kortcha, the work of the school has been conducted by her sister.

The American School for Girls at Monastir has been under the direct care of Miss Cole. Forty-seven pupils have been enrolled, twenty-nine of whom were boarders. Some of the orphans have been trained in the school, and others will probably be brought in as soon as they reach an age which will warrant it. ...

1906
96th Annual Report
Thomson Memorial Chapel, Williamstown, Massachusetts
October 9–12, 1906

Pages 51–52, 58
European Turkey Mission — Two serious problems confront the mission. One of these is that of the *Zornitza* and publication work. ... The other problem concerns relations to the Methodists. The missionaries are entirely

willing to cooperate with that mission in the *Zornitza*, in educational work, or in Albania, but the Methodist Mission feels that a necessary condition of cooperation is the opening of a preaching place in Sofia. ...

The Monastir Girls' Boarding School, the only evangelical school for girls in Macedonia, enrolled 51 pupils, 26 of them boarders. They represented 6 nationalities. The amount received for the support of the boarders was $378.40, an increase of $48.40 over last year. There were 2 American teachers and 4 native assistants. There was no graduation in 1906. At its annual meeting the mission rejected a proposition which had come from native sources for the transfer of the school to Salonica and for the use of Bulgarian rather than English as the language of the school.

Kortcha, in Albania, had regular preaching under Mr. Tsilka, returned from America. The average church and Sunday school attendance was 21, though the last of the year it was between 30 and 35. Two missionaries and as many native assistants as possible are needed for this Albanian work. The girls' school was reopened and permission given to use the Albanian language. The number of pupils was about 65 until persecution reduced it to 25. At the graduating exercises, when 2 were presented with diplomas, there were present most of the government officials, all the beys, and all the best families.

1907

97th Annual Report
Pilgrim Congregational Church, Cleveland, Ohio
October 9–11, 1907

Pages viii, xv
Persons under Appointment — Rev. and Mrs. Phineas B. Kennedy, European Turkey.

The missionaries about to depart for their fields were presented, and remarks were made by Rev. D. M. Rogers, Rev. A. W. Staub, Rev. and Mrs. P. B. Kennedy.

Page 5
Appointment of missionaries, European Turkey: Miss Inez L. Abbott, sailed August 24, from Montreal, to be associated with Miss Maltbie in the Girls' School at Samokov. Rev. and Mrs. Phineas B. Kennedy will probably sail in October, directly after the Board meeting.

Page 49
European Turkey Mission — The Kortcha Girls' Boarding School has had difficulties again with the government on account of the use of the Albanian language. The school was officially closed last February, though school work has not actually been stopped. The matter is in the hands of the embassy, and it is hoped that the outcome will be perfect freedom for work in connection with the school.

Mr. Tsilka has been holding English classes for boys. He reports increased interest in and attendance at the preaching services. The attendance has been 21; Sunday school, 21.

1908
98th Annual Report
Academy of Music, Brooklyn, New York
October 13–16, 1908

Pages 45–48
European Turkey Mission

Monastir — William P. Clarke, Ordained; Mrs. Martha G. Clarke, Miss Mary L .Matthews, Miss Mary M. Haskell.

Kortcha — Phineas B. Kennedy, Charles T . Erickson, Ordained; Mrs. Violet B. Kennedy, Mrs. Carrie L. Erickson.

This mission has been reenforced by the coming of Miss Inez L. Abbott, who has been assigned to Samokov. Rev. and Mrs. Phineas B. Kennedy, sent out for work in Albania, have been located at Kortcha; to this same station Rev. and Mrs. Charles T. Erickson have been commissioned.

Monastir — Rev. W. P. Clarke speaks of the year at this station as peculiar. Miss Cole spent the summer at Samokov, while Miss Haskell was spared from Samokov to take temporary charge of the orphanage at Monastir. The native pastor has been faithful in his work, and the church has been quickened, 6 having been received into its membership.

The Girls' Boarding School, for which Miss Cole reports, speaks of the excellent conduct of the scholars, 3 of whom graduated in June, 1907. More money has been paid by boarders than in any previous year, notwithstanding the increased cost of living. Of the 35 girl graduates from this school all were members of the church, and all but 2 are engaged in direct work for the mission.

Kortcha, heretofore an outstation of Monastir, is to be regarded as having become a station on March 26, 1908, on the arrival of Rev. and Mrs. Kennedy. These friends were detained at Salonica, not having been permitted to go into the interior. Mr. E. B. Haskell went to Kortcha in October last and opened a school; Mr. W. P. Clarke took his place in November, and remained there until the opening of the present year. During the summer of 1907 Mr. Tsilka was arrested and fined for not having closed the school, as ordered to do by the authorities, but after trial he was acquitted of this charge. Later on his house was searched and books and manuscripts were taken away; and though no evidence of disloyalty to the government was discovered, he was again arrested March 20, 1908, and was held in confinement until July 23, when that marvelous bloodless revolution occurred by which prison doors were opened and Mr. Tsilka was set free.

Salonica — The hard conditions under which the work has been carried forward for three or four years at this station remain much as heretofore. The revolutionary bands are maintaining an internecine strife, traveling has been unsafe, murders have been frequent, and trade much restricted. But the fact is noted that the people who are suffering under these trying circumstances are, to some extent at least, in their despair of obtaining relief from human sources, turning their faces toward divine things, and are seeking rest and support in God. These unfavorable conditions, which have prevailed throughout the district, have necessarily curtailed the touring to some extent; and yet it is reported that, aside from Mr. Haskell's 82 days spent in connection with affairs at Monastir and Kortcha, the missionaries and native laborers have spent a total of 251 days in touring. Colporters throughout the district have been encouraged by large sales and by a readiness to purchase the Christian literature brought them. The Scriptures have been circulated in no less than 21 different languages. New editions of the Scriptures, both the Old and New Testaments, are much needed.

Page 161

Report of the Treasurer — The cost of the missions as compared with the previous year increased $8,246.02, a part of this increase being due to the new work undertaken in Albania, supported by donations specified for such use.

1909

99th Annual Report
Plymouth Church, Minneapolis, Minnesota
October 13–15, 1909

Pages 46–51
European Turkey Mission

Monastir — William P. Clarke, Ordained; Mrs. Martha G. Clarke, Miss Mary L .Matthews, Miss Mary M. Haskell.

Kortcha — Phineas B. Kennedy, Ordained; Mrs. Violet B. Kennedy.

Residing at Tirana — Charles T. Erickson, Ordained; Mrs. Carrie E. Erickson.

Monastir — The work in Monastir was established in 1873. The population of the field can be considered 1,200,000. To work this field, in which there are 3 outstations beside the central station, there are 5 missionaries, including the single ladies, and 10 native laborers, including one ordained preacher. Regular meetings are held at five different places. There is one organized church not yet entirely self-supporting. The communicants number 103 and the adherents 133. The average attendance is 173. Seven were added to the church by confession during 1908. The 4 Sabbath schools have a membership of 113. The native contributions for the religious work amounted to $82.86.

The Boarding School [Monastir] —The Girls' Boarding School has enrolled a total of 30 pupils, 26 of whom were boarders. Of this number 28 are Bulgarians. Owing to illness Miss Cole has been obliged to leave the school. At the beginning of the school year 10 of the boarders were members of the church. The girls have contributed according to their ability to the Bulgarian Evangelical Society and to aid the Greek church in Salonica. A new American teacher is imperatively needed.

Kortcha— Mr. and Mrs. Erickson, with their children, have reenforced the Kortcha station, though at present they are located at Tirana. During the year a special deputation, consisting of Messrs. Peet, Thomson, and E. B. Haskell, was sent by the mission through Albania to select a location for a central station. They visited all the larger places in both the north and the south. They found the people just emerging from a long night of depression under a despotic government, and, with great national aspirations toward enlightenment and better civilization, open to any efforts educational and otherwise which the American missionary might desire to make. The deputation, while agreeing unanimously that Elbasan occupied a desirable central position both geographically and with respect to the great divisions of the people into Ghegs and Tosks, were still of the opinion that owing partly to the present want of accessibility it would be better for the status quo to be preserved for the time being. Accordingly the mission voted that Mr. and Mrs. Kennedy remain for another year at Kortcha and Mr. and Mrs. Erickson at Tirana.

The Kortcha station was established March 26, 1908. The field (Albania) has a population numbering upwards of two and a half millions. The force is comprised of 2 ordained missionaries and their wives and 1 unordained native preacher, with 4 teachers and 1 other worker. There is 1 place for holding religious services. There are 9 communicants, 1 having been added during the year. The average attendance at these services has been 34. The one Sabbath school has a membership of 20, though its average attendance has been 48. The people during the year have given £T. 10.06 ($44.26) for religious work and £T.59.15 ($260.26) for educational work. A small boys' school was started at Kortcha and run during the year, with an attendance of 35. There has also been a night school conducted three nights a week, with an attendance of 25. The attendance at the girls' school has been 70. So the work is slowly opening up, and it is hoped and expected that in these days of unparalleled opportunity in Albania the teachings and life of Jesus Christ will find their way in power through these missionaries and their institutions into the heart of the Albanian race.

The work under the Constitution — It is unnecessary to repeat what has been written and printed in so many forms and places about the changes wrought by the proclamation of the constitution in July, 1908.[4] The lifting of the censorship and of the restrictions on missionary touring and colportage in European Turkey is a cause for profoundest gratitude. It is too early yet to speak with confidence about the constitutional government. The first furor of the people over their newly granted liberty was detrimental to spiritual work among them. The constitutional clubs, wherever organized, have been holding their meetings on Sundays. For a time in some places courses of popular lectures on political and economic subjects on Sunday forenoons were given at about the time for preaching services. Women's auxiliaries to the clubs were organized and their meetings held Sunday afternoons. Sunday schools were even established in which illiterates were taught reading and writing and other rudimentary branches. Not only did these various attractions practically terminate the attendance of outsiders at the mission services, but they were also a sore temptation to the evangelical Christians to neglect divine worship. But now the Sunday lectures, club meetings, secular Sunday schools, etc., seem to be neglected and dying. Meanwhile the old, old story is reasserting its attractive power. The tide is turning. Congregations are increasing, and there is greater apparent interest in spiritual things than has been the case for years in Macedonia.

---

4 This refers to the reestablishment of the constitutional monarchy in the Ottoman Empire in 1908 (Sultan Abdul Hamid II was pressured to restore it after the Young Turk Revolution) (DH).

1910

100th Annual Report
Tremont Temple, Boston, Massachusetts
October 11–14, 1910

Pages 94–95
European Turkey Mission

Monastir — Miss Mary L. Matthews: *Principal of Girls' Boarding School.* Miss Mary M. Haskell: *Associate in the school; general work for women.*

Samokov — Robert Thomson, ordained: *Literary and educational work; acting principal of the Collegiate and Theological Institute.* Mrs. Agnes C. Thomson. John W. Baird, ordained: *Educational and evangelistic work.* Mrs. Ellen R. Baird. ...

Kortcha, Albania — Phineas P. Kennedy, ordained: *Educational and general evangelistic work.* Mrs. Violet B. Kennedy: *Educational work for girls and woman's evangelistic work.*

Elbasan, Albania — Charles T. Erickson, ordained: *General evangelistic work.* Mrs. Carrie E. Erickson.

Pages 96–102

At present there are practically three departments in the mission. The Bulgarian section, with its schools in Samokov and the publication work in the Bulgarian language, is carried on at Samokov and Philippopolis, with a kindergarten in Sofia. The Macedonian section centers in Salonica, with a second station at Monastir. The principal work of these stations is among the Bulgarians, and the young men in training for future service are sent across the line for education. In the last few years there has been developed a distinctively Albanian side of the work, although for many years the mission has been interested in the Albanian people and has done much for them, the school for girls in Kortcha having been carried on with great success. Two stations have recently been occupied by ordained missionaries sent out especially for the Albanian work, namely, Kortcha and Elbasan. This work is hardly yet well established, but the reception of the missionaries by the Albanians has been most encouraging. The station at Constantinople, which for many years was the publication center for this mission, has now had its work for the European Turkey Mission entirely transferred to Samokov. ...

The educational work of the mission centers in Samokov and Monastir. The Collegiate and Theological Institute at Samokov has for its object the giving of a general education to Bulgarian young men, and its scientific course covers seven years. During these seven years there is much Biblical study for all. Those who are contemplating entering directly into ministerial work take an eighth year which is purely theological ... During these fifty years over 800 students from all parts of Macedonia, Bulgaria, and Albania have come under its direct instruction.

In speaking of the educational work in Bulgaria we must not omit by any means the girls' boarding school at Monastir, which has been in operation since 1878, beginning as a day school. This school does for the girls of that part of the mission field what the Samokov school does for girls in Bulgaria. It is the only evangelical school for girls in Macedonia. Its course of study is four years, with plans contemplating the adding of one more year.

The Macedonian work, centering in the two stations of Monastir and Salonica, has been greatly hampered during the last few years by the unsettled political state of all Macedonia. These conditions are well-known to those who have kept themselves posted on the political movement in Turkey and so nothing need be added here. The retired Sultan, Abdul Hamid II, occupies his villa in Salonica. The city was the headquarters of the revolutionary movement before the overthrow of the old regime, and is looked upon at the present time as the stronghold of the new order. It was in Salonica that the new constitution was celebrated twenty-four hours ahead of the celebration in Constantinople. The field is a large one, with a population of over 2,000,000, mixed in character and method of operation, but of supreme importance. The Thessalonica Agricultural and Industrial Institute, in the suburbs of Salonica, is a growing institution incorporated under the laws of New York. Its object is to give to Macedonian boys a broad education that includes industrial together with spiritual and mental training.

No report of this mission would be complete without some special reference to Albania and the new work beginning among that most interesting and almost savage people. The field covered by the Albanian section of this mission is said to contain a population of 2,500,000. These people live in the mountains and represent in themselves the warlike forces of the Turkish empire. Albanian generals and commanders have exercised great influence in Turkey for the last century. The Albanians themselves are divided between the Greek Church and Mohammedanism, although it has been stated that many of those who profess Mohammedanism are not very stanch in their faith. The situation is greatly complicated by the fact that the Albanians long to be independent. The present difficulty with the Turkish government is based largely upon the overwhelming desire which they cherish for political freedom. They have given a most cordial reception to the missionary, due perhaps in large measure to their desire for modern education, accompanied by the fact that their native religions sit upon them rather lightly. There is a general feeling on the part of all of our missionaries who are cognizant of the situation that the time is ripe for the establishing of Christian schools in Albania, for opening medical work for them, and so for bringing to bear upon the race those Christian influences which have done so much in the reorganization of government through the introduction of the institutions of Christian civilization. It would be a sad commentary upon Christianity if this ancient and honorable race, when ready to receive the Christian missionary and the institutions which he represents, were left waiting in vain and compelled at last to turn away in disappointment. The mission carries on an extensive publication work in the Bulgarian language. The weekly evangelical paper, the *Zornitza*, has a wide and increasing circulation. Its constituency has been greatly extended since the inauguration of the new regime, as the paper has been permitted to circulate among the Bulgarians of Macedonia.. In addition to this, from the mission press at Samokov have come educational and religious books in increasing numbers. It is matter of history that since the attention of the mission was turned to Bulgaria the influence of its literary work has been widely extended over the nation's literature. The Bible itself, a New Testament commentary, a Bible dictionary, a Harmony of the Gospels, hymn books, and a treatise on Evidences of Christianity, beside scientific, philosophical, and historical text books of all classes and a vast deal of other literature, have been issued during the past few years.

Institutions of the European Turkey Mission:

Collegiate and Theological Institute, Samokov, Bulgaria — The only evangelical school for boys and young men of Bulgaria. It has 87 students, of whom 77 are boarders. It has an industrial self-help department equipped with a printing and a wood-working plant. There are 13 teachers. The full course covers eight years of study. The scientific course can be completed in seven years.

Girls' Boarding School, Samokov — There were 99 girls enrolled during the year, with 20 more in the kindergarten. The course of study covers six years.

The Zornitza — A weekly Bulgarian evangelical paper, published by the mission and circulating among all classes.

Kindergarten at Sofia — Has an attendance of 107, reaching the best classes in the capital of Bulgaria.

Girls' Boarding and High School at Monastir — The only evangelical boarding school for Bulgarian girls in Macedonia. It has an attendance of 47.

Thessalonica Agricultural and Industrial Institute, Salonica — Agriculture and various industries are taught to all its students. This institution is independent of the mission but in close cooperation, under the direction of Dr. J. H. House, its president. There has been an attendance of 51.

Girls' Boarding School at Kortcha, Albania — Fourteen boarders and 60 day scholars. The only evangelical school for Albanian girls.

Publication Department at Samokov — Printed 123,515 copies of books and pamphlets, with a total of 8,630,090 pages. Forty-seven different and separate publications were issued. One of these publications was the New Testament for the British and Foreign Bible Society.

Page 104
The missions in Turkey have had to deal with various races and languages as well as religions, some of the latter hostile to each other, all of which has greatly complicated the effort in every department. The six languages with which they have had most directly to deal are the Turkish,

Armenian, Greek, Bulgarian, Arabic, and Kurdish, to which is added in these later years the Albanian. Each one of these peoples, speaking a language of their own, has a religion different from that of all others, although the Greeks, Bulgarians, and Armenians are members of ancient Christian churches. These churches have had little in common except to regard each other with suspicion.

1911
101th Annual Report
Plymouth Congregational Church, Milwaukee, Wisconsin
October 10–13, 1911

Page 66
European Turkey Mission

Monastir (1873) — *William P. Clarke, ordained: General evangelistic and educational work. Mrs. Martha G. Clarke. Miss Mary L. Matthews: Principal of Girls' Boarding School. Miss Delpha Davis: Student of language and educational work.*

Kortcha, Albania (1908) — *Phineas B. Kennedy, ordained: Educational and general evangelistic work. Mrs. Violet B. Kennedy: Educational and work for women.*

Elbasan, Albania (1910) — *Charles T. Erickson, ordained: General evangelistic work. Mrs. Carrie E. Erickson.*

Page 73

Missions in Turkey — The American Board work, in all this area, centres in what are called mission stations, that is, points where American missionaries reside, and out from which they work in the surrounding regions. Counting Constantinople as one station — although missionaries live in different sections of the city, there are 27 American Board stations in this group of Missions. Of these 3 are In Bulgaria, 4 in Albania and Macedonia, 8 in the western section of Asia Minor, 7 in northern Syria and Cilicia, and 5 in the eastern part of the Empire, including Armenia and Koordistan.

Pages 100–101

Missions in Turkey, medical work — In speaking of the need of enlargement of the work, there is a great opportunity for opening new medical work in Albania ... In Albania, where work was opened only four years ago, there is a universal demand for a medical missionary and a hospital, to be established in Elbasan, which has been decided upon as the centre of the work. Albania has no modern practitioners of any kind, and the suffering of its people can hardly be imagined by one who has lived only in the land of physicians and hospital privileges. It is believed by those who understand the situation, that a missionary physician in Elbasan, with a modest equipment for caring for the sick, would greatly aid the work of evangelizing the people, and throw open the door of approach to them.

Page 103
Institutions of the Turkey Missions, European Turkey

Girls' Boarding and High School, Monastir — The only evangelical boarding school for Bulgarian girls in Macedonia. It had an attendance of 48, 24 in the regular course, 14 preparatory', 5 primary and 5 specials. Seven teachers, 6 being native and 1 American.

Girls' Boarding School at Kortcha, Albania — Total attendance of 70, 14 being boarders. Four graduates this year. The only evangelical school for Albanian girls.

Page 104
Institutions of the Turkey Missions, Western Turkey

International College (for boys), Smyrna — Total enrollment, 340. College department, 220; preparatory, 120. Greeks, 238; Armenians, 45; others, including Turks, Jews, Austrian, Albanian, English, French, German, American, etc., 57. Teachers, apart from missionaries and those mentioned as associated with the mission, 20.

1912

102nd Annual Report
Williston Church, Portland, Maine
October 8–11, 1912

Pages 76–77

War in Macedonia — As this report goes to the printer war is raging in Macedonia, the Balkan States, Montenegro, Bulgaria and Servia, together with Greece, having precipitated an attack upon Turkey. This is causing a suspension of all ordinary forms of missionary work in Bulgaria and the withdrawal of the missionaries in Macedonia until the fury of the conflict has passed. The leading cities of Bulgaria, Macedonia, and even Constantinople are under martial law. No one would dare predict whereunto this war may or may not lead. ...

The four missions of the American Board in Turkey confront a variety of conditions, owing to diversity of location and contact with different races. The European Turkey Mission has in itself widely different problems since one half of the mission is in Bulgaria, an independent kingdom, and the other half in Macedonia, the most disturbed section of all Turkey and probably the worst governed. Macedonia with its Albanian, Greek and Turkish elements openly and religiously hostile to each other, and the entire area the object of envy and jealousy by Bulgaria, Russia, Austria, Greece and Turkey, presents all the elements for discord and disorder of every character. Add to this the intense desire of the Albanians for a certain measure of autonomy in local government and we have conditions which are becoming more acute daily and which may not settle without the intervention of Europe.

Pages 80–82
Unoccupied Areas — If we reckon the number of missionaries and Christian workers in Turkey and take account of their general distribution over the entire country we might say with not a little complacence, that the territory is occupied from a missionary point of view. Compared with many other missionary countries it is very well occupied with Christian workers and with the institutions of the Gospel. But to those familiar with the details of the work, there appear great populous areas and classes and races living wholly without a practical knowledge of Jesus Christ.

To be more specific, Macedonia, stretching from the Adriatic on the West and extending to the Black Sea on the East, bordered by Bulgaria and other independent or partially independent states upon the North and the Aegean Sea and Sea of Marmora upon the South, and all thickly populated, has been occupied as a mission field for nearly three quarters of a century. And yet at the present time we have in all that country only five ordained missionaries, five missionary wives and two single women, with no missionary physician. There are only a few native workers with great stretches of country unentered and millions of people unreached. Within this dwell that powerful and historic race, the Albanians, for whom almost nothing was done until five years ago, and for whose, 2,000,000 souls we have now upon the ground only two ordained missionaries with their wives. All the eastern section of Macedonia, including the great and ancient city, Adrianople, is the field of but little Christian work. ...

Probably the Koords and the Albanians, here mentioned together, number not less than 4,000,000 souls and they include some of the most virile of the populations of Turkey. ...

While in Turkey there is a large and able force of workers trained from among the people, far more numerous than the missionaries themselves, nevertheless the fact remains that Turkey as a country is not efficiently occupied. It would require more than double the present working force to hold the country effectively for Christ and to be in a position to push the work with reasonable efficiency. Many new missionaries should be sent in at once for work through the medium of the Turkish language, as well as the Koordish and Albanian languages, none of which tongues have as yet taken an adequately important place in our Christian propaganda. In our work as now constituted we are not keeping the numbers of our missionary forces good, to say nothing of the call for advance.

Albanian Work — Some four or five years ago, two missionary families, financed by a special fund given for that exclusive purpose, were appointed to open Christian work in Albania. It was anticipated that the task would be a severe one costing a prolonged struggle and in this we have not been disappointed. Mr. and Mrs. Kennedy and Mr. and Mrs. Erickson have faced this opposition with self-forgetful heroism. Two places have been occupied, each an important centre in the country, Kortcha and Elbasan. In the former place a girls' school has been maintained for many years under Christian Albanian supervision.

The Turkish Government brought to bear upon this opening work all the forces of opposition at its disposal. Mr. and Mrs. Erickson were forcibly driven out of Tirana, their first place of residence, and during the year under review they were ejected from Elbasan and taken under guard to Monastir, where they were detained for several months. A site had been previously purchased at Elbasan for the missionary work, to which the Government declined to give title and later expropriated it for military purposes, returning the purchase money. A second piece was then purchased, the title to which is now a subject of negotiation. Mr. Kennedy held the situation at Elbasan while Mr. Erickson was away, although at the same time the Government was attempting to close out the work at Kortcha.

In spite of this opposition an encouraging beginning has been made. The experiment has shown that the Albanians are friendly, and in spite of their oppression by the Turks are ready to give the preacher of the Gospel a cordial welcome. While freedom for public services is yet withheld, the people have assembled in a private way in the hired house of the missionary in Elbasan, to the number of fifty persons at a service, with an average attendance of some thirty. At Kortcha the attendance has been larger, with a Sunday School on occasions numbering 200. The missionaries and Mr. Tsilka and Mr. Dako, American trained Albanian Christian workers, have found a warm welcome in other towns and cities visited, while the school at Kortcha is crowded beyond endurance, and a perpetual call comes up from Elbasan for the opening of a boys' school and a medical work there.

This new work demands immediate enlargement in the way of houses for the missionaries, proper accommodations for the schools at Kortcha and Elbasan, and provision for a medical work at the latter place. In all Albania there is no trained doctor, and all evidence goes to show that a Christian missionary physician would be universally welcomed by the Albanians and his influence practically unlimited.

In his report Mr. Erickson says: "The sooner the Christian Church realizes that the Christianity of Jesus Christ is a conquest and take to heart the task of saving society at least as seriously as they do their own comfort and enjoyment, the sooner will be wiped out the reproach of starving, dying nations like this one, and the sooner will be realized the city of tearless eyes where God himself is King."

Pages 93–95
Medical Work — The Western Turkey Mission has voted to favor locating a medical missionary in that old capital of the empire, Brousa, and the European Mission is urgent that a medical work should be opened at once in Elbasan, Albania....

Publication Work — As an illustration of a single phase seldom mentioned consider the amount of money passing though the hands of Mr. Peet, the treasurer of these four missions. When these figures are read one must bear in mind that the Treasurer is also the missionary adviser of the U. S. Embassy at the Porte, and the go-between for the transaction of any and all diplomatic missionary business; he is also the chairman of the Albanian Committee, a member of the Committee ad interim, etc. There passed though the office of the treasurer during the year 1911 the sum of $614,701.21.

1913
103rd Annual Report
First Congregational Church, Kansas City, Missouri
October 26–28, 1913

Pages 6–7
Minutes of the Annual Meeting — The following missionaries were introduced and spoke briefly: ... Mr. and Mrs. C. T Erickson, of Albania. ...

Monday Evening (October 27, 1913): Addresses were made by Rev. Charles T. Erickson, missionary to Albania; Miss Ellen M. Stone and Secretary Barton. ...

A special offering of $10,000 was made for work in Albania, and a telegram sent to the government there pledging a hospital in these terms: "The American Board of Missions, in Annual Meeting assembled, profoundly sympathizes with Albania in her struggle for national and religious liberty. May God speedily send peace, prosperity, and the triumph of national righteousness to you. Hospital pledged for Albania."

Pages 61-66
Stations: The Balkan Mission

Monastir (1873) —William P. Clarke, *ordained*: Evangelistic and educational work. Mrs. Martha G. Clarke. Miss Delpha Davis: Language study; acting-principal of the Girls' Boarding School.

Kortcha, Albania (1908) —

Elbasan, Albania (1910) — Phineas B. Kennedy, *ordained*: Evangelistic and educational work. Mrs. Violet B. Kennedy: Educational and work for women.

On furlough — C. Telford Erickson, *ordained*; Mrs. Carrie E. Erickson; Miss Mary L. Matthews.

Mr. and Mrs. Erickson have come to the United States in the interests of the work in Albania. Mr. and Mrs. Kennedy are at Elbasan temporarily. Miss Matthews has come home for furlough.

Turkey and the Balkan Mission, separation of missions Owing to the political changes that have taken place in Turkey during the last year, especially in the European section, we can no longer speak of four missions in Turkey. While there has been no formal action changing the name of what has hitherto been called the European Turkey Mission, already in the Rooms and in correspondence the work of the American Board in the Balkans, including Albania, has been referred to repeatedly as the Balkan Mission. Probably this will remain as the permanent name of the Mission. That being the case, when we refer hereafter to our Turkish Missions we shall mean the three missions to Turkey, namely, the Western, Eastern and Central Turkey Missions. The border line between the Balkan Mission and the Western Turkey Mission has not yet been decided upon. As Adrianople remains a part of the Turkish empire, it will probably continue to be included in the Western Turkey Mission. What remains, namely, the work in Bulgaria, Servia, Greece and Albania, will probably be called the Balkan Mission, and will require separate consideration in all reports hereafter.

Changes due to the war — While there has been no change in the location of the missionaries of the Board, the last year has witnessed a great change in the conditions under which their work is conducted. Early in the war in which the allies joined their forces against Turkey, Monastir was taken possession of by the Servians. Under the agreement signed by the Powers concerned, this city is to remain permanently a part of Servia. At about the same time Kortcha and Salonica were taken possession of by the Greek army, so that the American Board for the present has two stations under the Greek flag. A conference of the Powers in London has outlined the boundary for an independent Albania upon the north and east, although, at this writing, the southern boundary is still unsettled. This action of the Powers gives to Albania, Scutari on the north, which was the object of so much controversy throughout nearly the entire period of the war, Kortcha in the southeast section, which at this writing is still held by the Greeks, as well as Tirana, Elbasan and Durazzo, three places which have figured more or less prominently in the last five years, in connection with the American Board work in Albania.

The Servians early took possession of northern Albania, and soon after their arrival at Durazzo, Elbasan and Tirana, they arrested Mr. Erickson and Mr. Tsilka. Mr. Erickson, on December 10, was ordered to leave, with his family, within twenty-four hours after notice was served upon him, and Mr. Tsilka was kept in confinement for several weeks before he was given his liberty.

Mr. Erickson went to Switzerland, and then to London, until after the Powers had delimitated the northern section of independent Albania, when he returned and traveled extensively over the country, making investigations with a view to future occupancy of Albania for missionary purposes.

Mr. and Mrs. Kennedy remained at Kortcha after the Greeks had taken possession of the city for several weeks, but on April 24 they received orders to prepare to withdraw, and they were sent under Greek guard to Salonica. The reasons given by the Greeks for the expulsion of Mr. Kennedy were wholly unsatisfactory and without any ground. The Greek Government, however, after correspondence gave assurance to our State Department, that as soon as order was restored in Kortcha, Mr. Kennedy would be allowed to return. Although Kortcha falls within independent Albania as set apart by the European Powers, up to October 1 the Greeks have not withdrawn, and indications are many that they do not intend to do so. It remains to be seen what the outcome will be there.

In Salonica there was an entire suspension of every form of work as there was in Kortcha and Elbasan during the hostilities and even down to the present time, except that the missionaries gave themselves with great abandon to the work of relief for which there was boundless call. The refugees flocked into Salonica where Mr. Haskell and Mr. Cooper devoted their entire time and strength to relief work. While they have not been personally molested by the Greek authorities, the later development of their hostility to Bulgaria since 1868. Missions in Turkey has raised doubt as to whether the Greeks would allow any work to be carried on in Salonica, or in fact anywhere under the Greek flag, in the Bulgarian language, as there is also serious doubt as to whether any work in Kortcha or in any part of Albania under the Greek flag would be allowed to continue if the Albanian language was used. The Greek officials in Salonica have expressed themselves as not hostile to the work of the American mission, but they have given no assurance that that work will be allowed to continue.

In Monastir, under the Servian flag, the situation has not been so strained as in the south. The girls' school has not been hindered; in fact, while the city changed hands, the school did not lose a day but every session was held as usual. At the closing exercises of the school in June, Servian officials were present who seemed to be very much gratified with what they saw. They have shown no hostility to our work as yet, but they have not seemed to be favorable to the Bulgarians for whom our work is especially organized.

The Future — Just what form the future work of the American Board in this mission will assume is still uncertain, as is also the center from which that work will be carried on. The plan to develop an aggressive work in Albania under the earnest petition of the Albanians themselves is in process of formation. The Albanian people as a whole, numbering between two and three millions, are urgently requesting the American Board to open evangelistic, educational and medical work among them, as they are also calling for educational and Christian leaders. Rarely in the history of missions has such an opportunity come to any missionary society, or such a request from a Mohammedan people.

Mr. Kennedy has remained in Albania for the distribution of relief; a school for boys has been opened in Elbasan, and the endeavor is being made to secure the title to property purchased some three years ago in Elbasan for a mission compound. Reports have recently come that the Greeks have taken forcible possession of the girls' school in Kortcha, where the American Board has carried on a mission school for more than twenty years. This but indicates the hostile attitude that can be expected from the Greeks, while on the other hand the reception given by the Albanians but shows their friendliness and eagerness to cooperate with us in the execution of any and all plans for the development of work there.

Pages 81–82
The Balkans (European Turkey)

Girls' Boarding and High School, Monastir — The only evangelical boarding school for Bulgarian girls in Macedonia. Enrollment was 59, of whom about 24 were boarders. Besides the primary and preparatory grades, a new class taking a High School course was added. Eight graduated from this course. The regular course is now 5 years. The faculty includes 2 missionaries and 4 native teachers. The school was closed only for a day or two when the city was taken by the Servians. The closing of the national schools has sent an extra number of pupils to the mission school, especially in the lower grades.

Girls' Boarding School at Kortcha, Albania — The only evangelical school for Albanian girls. The roll at end of the year included 76 names, 15 being boarders and 7 Moslems. The Ladies' Literary Society reaches out of school bounds to give the elements of education to the women of Albania. Mr. and Mrs. Kennedy continued their oversight of the school until the city was taken by the Greeks and they were compelled to leave for Salonica. Mr. Kennedy had started a night school for boys. The future of the school waits on the outcome of the delineation of Albania and the general improvement of conditions following the war.

Page 85
The Balkans (Western Turkey)

Gedik Pasha School, Constantinople — The work of the school has been greatly strengthened by the securing of title to the property which is now occupied, a grant for its purchase having been given by the Woman's Board. The missionaries living near the school have rendered valuable assistance. The pupils enrolled were: Turks, 50; Albanians, 13; Persians, 7; Armenians, 79; Greeks, 44; Arab, 1; total, 194. Eight were graduated, several of them planning to continue their education in the American schools. In this school, as well as in others, the different nationalities live and work together in entire harmony. There is a strong faculty with 6 missionary teachers.

Page 209
Report of the Treasurer: New Obligations — About six years ago, through the generosity of two ladies who gave $30,000 for this purpose, the Albanian field was opened. Subsequently additional sums were contributed. This fund is now practically exhausted, only $73.13 being in hand. The work as at present established cost the past year $4,926.40, and an enlargement of the enterprise in the immediate future is imperative.

1914
104th Annual Report
First Congregational Church, Detroit, Michigan
October 13–16, 1914

Page 6
Mr. E. H. Pitkin proposed to raise a fund of $1,000 for Albania by offering $100 and $250 more was then pledged.

Pages 16–17
Albania, Shansi, and Van Appeals — This year there have been three special appeals of considerable prominence. At the last annual meeting, held in connection with the National Council, under the thrilling appeal of Rev. C. Telford Erickson and at the instance of a home missionary pastor, a special fund was started for new work in Albania, $10,000 being raised on the spot for a hospital building. Mr. Erickson at his own request was set apart to solicit

additional funds toward an authorized budget of $63,600. The story of his success is well known. His addresses throughout the country, from New England to the Pacific Coast, resulted in the securing of gifts and subscriptions considerably surpassing the above amount, a good many friends of other denominations coming forward to help. ... For quick financial response and the speedy coming forward of the needed workers, Albania and Shansi [China] stand out with a good deal of distinctness in our minds. It would seem that, aside from maintaining the stated work of the Board, our constituents desire us to engage in such new enterprises.

Pages 30–31
Report from the Interior District for Year 1913–1914
A number of returned missionaries have aided in the general work of cultivation. Rev. C. Telford Erickson, of Albania, has spoken with marked effect in a number of states. ...

During the entire year Rev. LeRoy H. Stafford, under appointment of the Board to Albania, has assisted the Secretary in the Chicago office and field with encouraging results. Early in the season he organized or assisted in organizing some thirty mission study classes, with a membership of about 500, for which several hundred copies of "What Next in Turkey?" were sold. He has likewise visited quite a number of our churches, associations, and colleges, and has variously aided in the work of this field. An able young man has been secured to be the associate of the Secretary in this large district, just as soon as the way opens for Mr. and Mrs. Stafford to go to Albania.

The Secretary's time has been fully occupied in field and campaign work, visiting churches and associations, holding interviews, with candidates, planning missionary appointments, conducting correspondence, and superintending the various details of our work in this field. Several weeks early in the year he was occupied as team leader of two groups of conferences, conducted under the auspices of the United Missionary Campaign. These were held in three states of this district, Mr. Erickson, of Albania, and Dr. Newell, of Japan, rendering valuable aid. Similar interdenominational conferences were held in other parts of the district.

Pages 61–62
The Balkan Mission

Monastir (1873) —William P. Clarke, *ordained*: Evangelistic and educational work. Mrs. Martha G. Clarke. Miss Delpha Davis: Acting-principal of the Girls' Boarding School.

Kortcha, Albania (1908) —

Elbasan, Albania (1910) —

On furlough — C. Telford Erickson, *ordained*; Mrs. Carrie E. Erickson; Phineas B. Kennedy, *ordained*; Mrs. Violet B. Kennedy.

Mr. and Mrs. Erickson have started back to Albania, but are detained in Europe on account of war conditions. ...

Several new recruits have been appointed with a view to strengthening the work in Albania, but are detained here on account of war conditions. These are Mr. and Mrs. LeRoy H. Stafford, for general evangelistic work; Mr. Charles H. Riggs, an agriculturist; Miss Cecile B. Bowman, for educational work; and Miss Hilda Hawley, a nurse.

Pages 67–72
The Balkan Mission — It will take some time to become thoroughly familiar with what constitutes the Balkan Mission ... This includes work carried on in Greece, centering at Salonica, work in new Servia with the central station at Monastir, work in Albania on the Adriatic, in Durazzo, Elbasan, Tirana and Kortcha, and the old Bulgarian Mission. ...

In Albania the situation has been just about as bad as it could be so far as the local government is concerned. Soon after the meeting of the American Board in Kansas City, where $10,000 was raised for building a hospital in Albania, Prince William of Wied was chosen by a London conference to be the ruler of new Albania. He made Durazzo the seat of his government. For one reason or another he did not succeed in establishing and maintaining order, and during his brief reign Albania was swept by various revolutions or uprisings, which ultimately resulted in his withdrawal and the leaving of Albania in its former condition, or even worse.

During all this period Mr. and Mrs. Kennedy remained in the country, except for a few weeks when they went into

Bulgaria for the annual meeting of the Mission and for a surgical operation, until after the European war broke out, when it became impossible to secure funds. Then it was that Mr. and Mrs. Kennedy entered upon the furlough that had been granted them a year before, but which they had refused to take in the face of the great need of their beloved Albanians.

Mr. Erickson remained in this country until into the spring, when he spent some time in Switzerland, in interesting others in the Albanian work. Considerable funds have been paid in and others pledged for work in Albania as soon as order is restored and the work can be entered upon with safety. In the meantime Mr. and Mrs. Kennedy have come home for their much-needed furlough, and Mr. Erickson is in Italy becoming acquainted with the large number of Albanians living in that country, and getting ready to go back into Albania when the proper time arrives. Mr. and Mrs. Stafford, Miss Bowman and Mr. Riggs have been appointed to Albania, the latter for agricultural and industrial work, while Miss Hawley, a trained nurse, is in England under appointment, waiting for opportunity to enter upon the work. A physician is in sight, although he has not yet been appointed to Albania, but there is expectation that he is the man we have been seeking for the place. We have, therefore, a force ready to enter Albania when the proper time comes to begin the work there. All of those that have been under appointment are now in special preparation, improving the delay to the best advantage of the work.

In the meantime a special board of trustees has been formed for the Kyrias School in Kortcha, thus relieving the Board of the responsibility and care of the school. Mr. Dako, who was formerly connected with that school, after taking his degree in Oberlin, and Miss Kyrias, also after study in Oberlin, have returned, and begun work in Kortcha, but, owing to the revolutionary condition of the country, were finally compelled to withdraw. They are waiting for opportunity to go back.

All these conditions show most emphatically the necessity of Christian work for the Albanians. There is every probability that, as soon as the war is over, and Southeastern Europe settles down to orderly procedure, there will be no difficulty in the way of missionaries entering Albania and laying the foundation for future work there. The experiences of the last year have shown that there is great ability, strength, and virility in the Albanian people, and an approachableness which promises much for the future.

Of the Balkan group of missions that in Bulgaria is on the whole the most promising and progressive just now. There seems to be no hindrance to its rapid development in every department of work. The Albanian situation is still held in abeyance, while the new work under the Greek and Servian flags is in its earlier stages without sufficient data yet to decide what its future will be.

Pages 90–92

Girls' Boarding and High School, Monastir — In spite of war and the interruptions consequent thereon, the work of the school has gone forward without interruption. Miss Davis had oversight of the school during the absence of Miss Matthews. Certain changes have been made, such as the giving up of Bulgarian as the main language of instruction and the substitution of Servian as the accompanying tongue. English also is receiving increased attention and will doubtless assume greater importance as a means of instruction. The boys' department is increasing in attendance, and the time is near at hand when a man must be put in charge. The growth of the day school has been phenomenal, an increase of 18 5 per cent., largely due to the closing of the Bulgarian and Greek schools. A kindergarten was opened at the request of parents, with an initial attendance of 20. The statistics show a faculty of 10, including 2 missionary teachers. The total attendance was 115 , divided into 13 boarders and 102 day pupils. Besides these there were 69 in the boys' department, making a grand total of 184. By nationality they include 131 Bulgarians, 35 Greeks, 6 Jews, 3 Albanians, and some others. Since the beginning 47 have graduated from the school, of whom 36 have taught more or less continuously in the mission schools.

Girls' Boarding School, Kortcha, Albania — No full report can be made for this school, owing to the interruptions of the Balkan wars. As indicated in the last report, there was a full attendance in the early part of the war, and Mr. and Mrs. Kennedy maintained the work as long as they remained in Kortcha. When they were expelled, in April, 1913, the school was continued for a time by Mrs. Dako, but was closed when she was compelled to leave after the occupation of the city by the Greek army. Although included in our report as a part of the mission work, the school is now under a separate board of trustees.

Boys' Boarding School, Elbasan, Albania — The boys' school was maintained as far as possible, after the withdrawal of Mr. Erickson, and Mr. and Mrs. Tsilka. In the course of their year's work Mr. and Mrs. Kennedy spent several months at Elbasan and assisted in the work of the school.

Page 228

Albanian Funds —At the annual meeting of the Board in Kansas City, pledges for a new hospital in Albania were made amounting to $10,373. Cash receipts prior to September 1, 1914, on account of these pledges were $9,113.17. A single gift of $15,000 has also been received for the purposes of a boys' school. A plan has been proposed for an extensive enlargement of our missionary work in Albania, which if adopted will involve an expenditure of an additional $100,000; but the total receipts for Albanian work during the year, not including those for the hospital and the boys' school, were only $4,545.67, while the current expenses of the year as now conducted, including the support of the two missionary families under appointment, were $5,519.46.

1915

105th Annual Report
First Congregational Church, New Haven, Connecticut
October 26, 1915

Pages 69–70
Mr. and Mrs. Erickson are still in Europe waiting for an opportunity to return to the mission, and Mr. and Mrs. Kennedy and Miss Baird are in this country, waiting also. ... Miss Hawley, the nurse who was secured for work in Albania has found an opportunity for service at Monastir, having first spent several months at Salonica.

Pages 94–96
The work of the Balkan Mission has gone on about as last year. Mr. and Mrs. Kennedy came home on furlough, and Dr. and Mrs. Erickson have been waiting in Italy for opportunity to get into Albania. Dr. Erickson made a brief tour in Albania, but has not been permitted to begin any regular work. He has devoted himself largely to work in Italy among Albanians there, and in getting acquainted with the situation. ...

Probably in the history of the American Board, a report for the year has never been written that was so completely taken up with questions gathering about war and atrocities. Never before have such a large proportion of the missionaries of the Board been for twelve months and more engaged in questions not primarily and directly missionary, but in questions gathering about the saving of the people for whom they were at work and the institutions which they had built up in the country. Never have missionaries made a more enviable record for themselves and for the cause they serve, or been able more completely to seize upon the situation and impress, through unusual conditions, the purity, simplicity and power of the Gospel of Jesus Christ. We face another year full of uncertainties, but with an unwavering confidence that the Lord will use the events of this year for the establishment of his eternal kingdom in the heart of the Turkish empire.

Page 103
Collegiate and Theological Institute, Samokov — The greatest need of the school as stated in the last report was Government recognition. That happy event is now consummated and the graduates of the Institute are on a par with those from the Government Gymnasium. A better class of students will now apply for admission and graduates who go to the University will take up positions of influence in the country. The diploma from the Institute having the Government stamp upon it will now be recognized as having full value.

1916

106th Annual Report
First Congregational Church, Toledo, Ohio
October 24, 1916

Pages 73–74
The Balkan Mission — *In Italy* — *Charles T. Erickson, D. D., ordained: Mrs. Carrie E. Erickson General work and study.*

Mr. and Mrs. Erickson are in Italy ready to go over to Albania when the way opens. After two years in America Mr. and Mrs. Kennedy of Albania have joined the Salonica station.

Pages 90–91
International College at Smyrna — It is a significant fact that this year completes twenty-five years of uninterrupted service rendered by President MacLachlan to the college. President MacLachlan is its founder and first and only president. No other collegiate institution in Turkey has had a more successful career or a more rapid development than has this college within the last few years under the wise and strong leadership of its president. ... It is an interesting fact that eleven nationalities and religions are represented in this student body: 83 were Greeks; 68 Armenians; 26 Turks; 19 Jews; to which were added English, Arabs, Austrians, Americans, Dutch, Albanians, and Poles; 164 of the members were Ottoman, the others scattering among eight different nations. It is an interesting feature of the

school that ten of these pupils were citizens of nations at war with Turkey, and yet they were allowed to continue their studies undisturbed.

Page 103

Albania — The work of the American Board in Albania has been at a standstill, no missionary having been able to get into the country during the entire year. Mr. and Mrs. C. Telford Erickson have remained in Italy in touch with a large number of Albanians in that country, and Mr. and Mrs. Phineas B. Kennedy, after working among Albanians in the United States, have returned, as above reported, to Salonica.

1917

107th Annual Report
Memorial Hall, Columbus, Ohio
October 15, 1917

Pages 62–63
The Balkan Mission

Monastir (1873) —Miss Mary L. Matthews: Principal of Girls' Boarding School; relief work.

Kortcha, Albania (1908) — Phineas B. Kennedy, ordained: General station and school work. Mrs. Violet B. Kennedy: Work for women; educational work.

Elbasan, Albania (1910) —

In Italy — Charles T. Erickson, D. D., ordained; Mrs. Carrie E. Erickson: General work and study.

Rev. John W. Baird died in Los Angeles, California on November 9, 1917. Mr. and Mrs. Erickson are still in Italy where he has been studying Italian and waiting for some development in the Albanian situation which may suggest an opening for service. After nine months in Salonica, Mr. and Mrs. Kennedy were able to return to Kortcha on September 21, 1917. Mr. and Mrs. Clarke of Monastir are now located in Salonica and Dr. and Mrs. Haskell of Philippopolis have been transferred to Samokov.

Pages 68–70
The Balkans — From the Bulgarian side of the Balkan Mission practically nothing has been received during the entire year. The American Government does not accept mail for the Balkans and communications from there are not allowed to come through. It is only indirect and remote reports showing that the missionaries are well and the work going on as well as could be expected under the untoward war conditions that prevail that have come to us at all. Communication with Salonica, however, has been more open. The work there has been unusually active, both in the agricultural school at the farm and at the station in Salonica. The entire mission force has been on the ground, as reported a year ago, with the addition of Mr. and Mrs. Kennedy who returned during the year. There has been a great demand upon the missionaries for relief work. ...

Mr. and Mrs. Kennedy, after a brief period spent at Salonica, upon the call of the Albanian Governor of Kortcha and with the approval of the French military authorities and the United States Consul and the station at Salonica, went to Kortcha to reopen the work there. Their going was assisted by the French military authorities and their welcome was all that could be desired. Several communications have come from them since their arrival and there is no indication of any hindrance whatever to their opening the school and going on with the work. There is great need for funds to put the school thoroughly upon its feet.

The situation in Monastir has remained about the same during the year and that is just about as bad as can be. Miss Matthews has chosen to remain on there alone, although Mr. and Mrs. Clarke were compelled to withdraw to Salonica, thus reinforcing the Salonica station but leaving Miss Matthews without any missionary associate. The school for the greater part of the year has not been in session, but evidently there has been a considerable number of girls and women in the home with Miss Matthews. The premises have been under bombardment repeatedly and the buildings have been somewhat injured by the explosion of bombs and shells either within the buildings or in the immediate neighborhood. It is evident that Miss Matthews' life has been in peril at times; in fact, while she was conversing with an English woman', the mother of one of the British officers, a fragment of a shell exploded near by fatally wounding the English woman while Miss

Matthews was uninjured. She has been urged to join her colleagues in Salonica, but has chosen to stay on in the midst of the peril that surrounds her there. There have been other Europeans in the city with whom she has been associated, but none of her missionary colleagues.

The missionaries seem strong in their conviction that when the war conditions have passed, the work in the Balkans will be more promising than ever before. The relation between the missionaries and the Bulgarian Government and officials has continued cordial and friendly. Bulgaria has not, up to the present time, broken diplomatic relations with the United States and it is not expected, if that step were taken, that it would materially affect the standing and work of the missionaries, who are recognized everywhere as nonpolitical and non-partisan.

Mr. and Mrs. Erickson have remained in Italy, Mr. Erickson assisting in some of the general evangelistic work in that field and keeping in touch as far as possible with the situation in Albania.

During the year two disastrous fires have seriously affected Monastir and Salonica, although in neither case were the mission premises injured. The fire in Salonica came very near the mission house, but it was spared, although the missionaries removed many of their effects. These fires have added much to the distress and suffering in both cities and have put an additional strain and burden upon the missionary body.

Page 87

Girls' Boarding School, Kortcha, Albania — Closed for the time in Albania by war conditions. Not under Board supervision any longer but controlled by a separate Board of Trustees with headquarters at Oberlin. Mr. and Mrs. Kennedy have returned to Kortcha, and are reopening the school.

Boys' Boarding School, Elbasan, Albania — Closed at the time of the Balkan wars and not yet reopened, for obvious reasons.

1918

108th Annual Report
First Church of Christ, Hartford, Connecticut
December 10, 1918

Page 160
The Balkan Mission

Monastir (1873) —*Miss Mary L. Matthews: Principal of Girls' Boarding School; relief work.*

Kortcha, Albania (1908) — *Phineas B. Kennedy, ordained: General station and school work. Mrs. Violet B. Kennedy: Work for women; educational work.*

Elbasan, Albania (1910) —

Outside the Mission — *(Italy) Charles T. Erickson, D. D., ordained.*

Page 167

The Balkans — The way has not yet opened for the Ericksons to return from Italy to Albania. The Albanian nation has sustained a great loss in the death by influenza of Rev. Gregory Tsilka, one of the most prominent and devoted workers for his people. Rev. and Mrs. Kennedy have kept up preaching services and a small school at Kortcha. Early in October Mr. Kennedy underwent a successful operation on an abscess near his right kidney. French army surgeons did splendid work for him. It seems appropriate here to make thankful acknowledgment of services rendered our missionaries at Salonica, Monastir and Kortcha by surgeons of the British and French expeditionary forces who for over three years generously and fraternally responded to every call upon them in their line. And thanks are due not only to surgeons but others in these forces. Mr. Brewster writes, "We never can tell all the British have done for us, high and low."

Page 177

INSTITUTIONS OF THE BALKAN AND TURKEY MISSIONS

Girls' Boarding and High School, Monastir, Serbia — Supported by the Women's Board of the Interior. After the Balkan wars Monastir passed from the control of the Turkish to that of the Serbian government; was held by Bulgaria for a year during the Great War: then retaken by Serbia. The school has been closed for over two years, but the premises served as a refuge for orphans and others.

Miss Matthews remained heroically at her post, occupied with various kinds of relief work. The language of the school being English, the new popularity of that language in the district will give the institution great opportunities after peace is signed and the partially wrecked buildings restored. Its former teaching force of 10, including 2 Americans, will be inadequate to the new conditions.

Girls' Boarding School, Kortcha, Albania — Formerly supported by the W. B. M. I., but now under a separate Board of Trustees. After being closed for some years the school was reopened on a small scale by Rev. and Mrs. P. B. Kennedy in 1918. Girls were taught in the forenoon and boys in the afternoon. Political conditions still are very unsettled and the future wholly uncertain.

Boys' Boarding School, Elbasan, Albania — Closed at the time of the Balkan wars and not yet reopened, for obvious reasons.

1919
109th Annual Report
Park Congregational Church, Grand Rapids, Michigan
October 22–23, 1919

Page 15
Higher education on mission fields — In Turkey will arise large demands for funds in connection with our educational plants. Armenian orphans must be educated

whether an Armenian State is established or not. Turks and Kurds, Bulgarians and Greeks, Albanians and Serbians will turn to us for education. We desire to give them education in an atmosphere permeated with the spirit of Christ—that spirit of service which alone can make a decent civilization.

Pages 29–32
Turkey and the Balkans: political uncertainties — So, then, the Allies are still marking time. Nothing like a League of Nations is actually assured. Political boundaries in the field abroad are still unsettled. Greece, Albania, Bulgaria, not to say Serbia, are struggling hard to secure their own special terms. Constantinople has not yet been neutralized. No mandatory has been set up for Turkey. The Armenians are not yet assured of their own government or of their own boundaries. Czechoslovakia, Jugo-Slavia, and other newly organized states add to this "balkanization" peril. ...

Again, there is the situation in the Balkans that has been forced upon us during the year as perhaps never before. Considerable pressure has been brought to bear upon the Board by the Greco-Serbian group, by the Albanians, and indirectly by the people from Bulgaria. The very fact that some of our missionaries in Salonica were arrested by the Greeks on the false charge of pro-Bulgarian activities proves the intensity of the racial jealousies that prevail in that Balkan cockpit. The mere dismissal of the missionaries has not lessened the significance of the struggle. What shall the American Board do toward giving the jealous peoples of the Balkans a spirit of cooperation? How can we help avoid the "balkanization" peril and produce those political, economic, and international foundations that are necessary for the settlement of all problems? This is morally and spiritually a task that seems superhuman. We realize now, as never before, the impossibility of solving the question of tyranny and intolerance in Turkey. Even the Armenian is inclined to take advantage of the Turk when he has the latter in his power, and the Greek himself seems to be showing as much of an unchristian feeling toward the Moslem. How can we help inject into the minds of the millions of the Levant a spirit of tolerance and of love? This is our task and a sobering one, it seems.

Page 72

Treasurer's Report, Miscellaneous Funds

Albanian Hospital Fund ($11,269.86); Albanian Medical Work Fund ($298.08); Albanian School Fund ($17,262.49).

1920

110th Annual Report
First Congregational Church, Marietta, Ohio
October 12–15, 1920

Pages 33–34

Survey of the Fields, The Balkan Mission — We use the name "Balkan Mission" for want of a better term. The four distinct nationalities included in this mission group, politically and racially, have little in common. By blood, the Serbs and the Bulgars are relatives, but by the fortunes of war that blood has become bad. The Greeks and the Bulgarians and the Serbs and the Bulgarians are perhaps the nearest hostile to each other, but it is not anticipated that this will eventuate in any outbreak, but the reverse. This group of stations cannot be organized into a compact mission, owing to national difficulties. In Albania, Mr. and Mrs. Kennedy have held on alone in Kortcha, which has changed hands during the year, passing from Greek to Albanian control. This has made communication difficult with the outside world. They have conducted a school for both boys and girls, kept up regular preaching service with Sunday school, Christian Endeavor Society, and a woman's organization. The boys and young men are eager to study. All available space in the buildings is occupied for school and religious services, and still the people come.

Mr. Kennedy, writing in May, says: "How these Albanians love America! They have their faces towards civil and religious light. These fields are white and ready." A new missionary family is immediately demanded, to be associated with the Kennedys for a year before they must retire, on account of greatly impaired health ...

Monastir is the only station of the American Board in Serbia. A few months ago the governor of that district urged that the Board open two more stations in Serbia at more central points, at the same time protesting against lessening the work there. The city suffered much, during the war, from fire and bombardment, and the mission premises and the church were hit by more than a dozen high-explosive shells; yet no one on the premises was injured. Two new appointees have been sent out to relieve Miss Matthews, and an ordained man is now imperatively needed to take supervision of the evangelistic work among the churches. This is the first missionary work conducted in Serbia by the American Board, and has been begun by Serbia taking over one of our missionary stations. ...

The Balkan field is upon the borders of Europe, and covers what has been a political storm center. Our mission occupies a place of surpassing importance, and in the judgment of many, of vital significance. We are there and well intrenched in the confidence of all classes, and are in a position to advance along every department of work, if only the men and the funds can be supplied. Did not the Lord place the Board in these important fields for a time like this?

Pages 56–57
Conclusion — The tendency in all fields is to settle down again to normal conditions, but not to return to a prewar status. The minds of the most backward races have experienced an awakening that precludes the possibility of a continuance of preceding stages of indifference and inaction. A new world of international consciousness has come into being and is rapidly becoming indigenous everywhere. The Albanian, the Georgian, the Turk, the Arab, the Indian, the Chinese, the Moro, not to mention the tribes and races of Africa and many other countries,

have awakened from the lethargy of centuries and are beginning to think of themselves as fellow-members of a common human race. "Rights," "privileges," "needs," "opportunity," as well as "responsibility" are terms that are finding place in strange languages, and are beginning to spur men on to longings and strivings hitherto little known or even dreamed. These aspirings and awakenings from within are vastly more significant than any external appearances of modernism. The soul of Asia and Africa is beginning to pulsate with new life, and we are entrusted with the commission to make that heart-beat harmonize with the great heart of our Lord Jesus Christ. We touch these peoples at a thousand centers. Shall virtue pass from us to them until they are healed?

1921

111th Annual Report (the first of two reports for 1921)
Harvard Congregational Church, Brookline, Massachusetts
October 18–20, 1921

Pages 62–63

The Balkan Mission — There is always something new in the Balkans. The missionary work in Servia and Albania is in the process of being transferred from the supervision of the American Board. This makes a large reduction in the area formerly covered by the Balkan Mission. At the same time, it concentrates our work in two very strong centers, Salonica in Greece, and Sofia in Bulgaria.

The stations and outstations in Servia, once occupied by the American Board are not being given up; they are being turned over to a Board with larger resources and with eager enthusiasm. At the same time, the change harmonizes with the desires of the Governments concerned. It always looks suspicious to one of the Balkan Governments to have an organization working on the boundary and in a neighboring state. Since the Methodist Board already was operating in Servia and since Monastir now lies in Servia, it made for harmony in relations with the Government to transfer the Monastir station to the same Board that was conducting work in other parts of the country. Similarly, Kortcha, Albania, is isolated from Salonica by a national boundary, so it is hoped that the work there and in the whole Albania field will be undertaken by our sister denomination. Perhaps the most potent reason for the change is the disadvantage of having a station isolated from other stations in language. It was for this reason that Mardin, the only Arabic speaking center of the Eastern Turkey Mission, was transferred to the Presbyterian Board. If the work at Monastir had been continued by the American Board, it would have required for this one station alone the establishment of a training center and a press using the Servian language. But now the efficiency of service in Servia is increased by concentrating the publication and educational work for the whole of the country. The definite responsibilities of the Methodist Board will begin on January 1, 1922. There now remain in the Balkan Mission but two elements, the Greek and the Bulgarian.

1921–1922

112th Annual Report
Meetings in Los Angeles, California and Evanston, Illinois
July 7–8, 1921 and October 24, 1922

Pages 60–61

Location and Special Work of Missionaries: Bulgarian Mission — The work in Albania and Servia having been discontinued, and that in Salonica and Greece transferred to the Western Turkey Mission, the report for this year is confined to Bulgaria. Mr. and Mrs. Ostrander and Miss Douglass have returned to Samokov leaving Mr. and Mrs. King the only missionaries on furlough. They will not return to Bulgaria until building operations begin. Mr. and Mrs. Kennedy of Albania and Miss Mary Haskell of Bulgaria have withdrawn from the service of the Board. Rev. Theodore T. Holway was reappointed, and Mrs. Holway appointed, in September 1922 and they are now in Philippopolis. Mr. John F. Stearns has joined the faculty in the Institute for a three year term. Mr. and Mrs. Markham have been transferred from Samokov to Philippopolis. The untimely death of Rev. Lyle D. Woodruff on June 14, 1922, took from the ranks a loved and efficient worker.

Pages 68–69

The Balkan Mission — There has been some discussion as to whether what was formerly the European Turkey Mission, later the Balkan Mission, should not be christened again the Bulgarian Mission. It is already known that the American Board has passed over to the Methodist Board all of the work which it formerly had in Serbia. The one station passed over was the station of Monastir, so that the American Board has now no mission work in Serbia.

The American Board was not able to develop or even to continue the small work that was begun in Albania fifteen years ago, and it did not seem fair for the American Board to hold on to Albania as one of its mission fields unless it was able more fully to develop the work. We have had only two missionary families in Albania from the beginning. Mr. and Mrs. Erickson retired three years ago and Mr. and Mrs. Kennedy came home this last year on account of Mr. Kennedy's ill health. The American Board has felt that it could not carry on the work in Albania and develop it as that most needy and promising field should be developed. Therefore it was decided not to continue the Albanian work as an American Board mission. But the suggestion has been made to the Methodist and the Presbyterian Board of Missions that a united mission be opened in Albania. The American Board holds some funds that have been contributed purely for educational and medical work in Albania which will be available under a joint mission. That matter is now under consideration. In the meantime the American Board has no work in Albania.

The Bulgarian Mission and the Western Turkey Mission, in view of the political conditions, have voted asking that Salonica be temporarily transferred to the Western Turkey Mission because there are no political, commercial or any other relations existing between Salonica, which is under the Greek flag, and Bulgaria. This question is still pending before the Prudential Committee. If Salonica is transferred to the Western Turkey Mission, it will be a temporary move pending the settlement of political questions in the Near East, but primarily for conveniences of administration. That will bring Salonica directly into touch with Constantinople rather than with Sofia, Bulgaria. The contacts with Constantinople are direct and regular, but very indirect and irregular with Bulgaria, with nothing in common between the two fields. Therefore our former European Turkey Mission, or the Balkan Mission, will become simply the Bulgarian Mission.

Pages 76–77
Albania: Girls' Boarding School, Kortcha (Balkans) —
This has passed quite recently with the whole of the work in Albania from the management of the American Board to the Methodist Mission in Bulgaria.

1923

113th Annual Report
Municipal Auditorium, Springfield, Massachusetts
October 19, 1923

Pages 58–59
Constantinople, Gedik Pasha School — Founded 1880 by Miss E. J. Gleason. ... There were 97 boys, 120 girls; 106 Armenians, 60 Turks, 41 Greeks, 6 Persians, 2 Bulgarians, 1 Albanian, 1 Arab. The largest class in the history of the school— 17, graduated last spring. ... A school for refugees, recorded as a branch of this school, was opened this year in the Gedik Pasha Evangelical Church with an enrollment of 72.

1924

114th Annual Report
Central Church, Providence, Rhode Island
October 21–23, 1924

Page 28
Report of the Prudential Committee for the Home Department, for the Year Ending August 31, 1924: Twenty-two years—years of unparalleled opportunity as the world swings open to the approach of Christ—and the Congregational churches of America order no advance! If Albania be cited as an exception, it is an exception which gives point to the barrenness of the record, since the work

in Albania, inaugurated as a result of individual gifts, was abandoned when it became apparent that the churches would not undertake the needed additional expense.

Index

Abbott, Inez, 110–111

Agricultural School of Kavaya (Kavaja), xv

Albania, boundaries of, 135, 139; need for a mission to, 74

Albanian Bible, xi–xii, 74

Albanian Evangelical Mission, xv

Albanian grammars and school books, xii, 81

Albanian language, descriptions of, 77; forbidden by the government, 107; not used for liturgy, xi

Albanian nationalism, xi

Albanian Protestant Movement xviii, new branch of Albanian historiography, xvi-xix

Albanians, descriptions of, 77, 115, 120–121; genuine interest in the Gospel, 75–77; interest in accepting Protestantism, 89, 137–138; love for America, 160; as Moslems, 31; soldiers, 6; students, 76–78

alphabets, xii, 88, 91

American Board of Commissioners for Foreign Missions, vii; annual meetings, xvi-xvii; Balkan Mission (map), xii-xiii; development of, xviii; discontinuation of Albanian work, 164–165, 167–168; offering of 10,000 USD for an Albanian hospital, 133; offering of 15,000 USD for a boys' school, 147; its mission, ix, 1, 106

American Collegiate and Theological Institute (Samokov), 56, 60, 68, 72, 78, 81, 83–84, 119, 122; government recognition of, 149; graduates preaching in Albania, 83; student missionary work, 50

Anderson, Rufus, 8

Armenians, 16–17, 24, 25, 31, 33, 38–39, 46, 124, 126, 139, 150, 157–159, 167

Baird, Agnes Mary, helping at the girls' school in Monastir, 79, 148

Baird, Ellen, organizes missionary society for girls, 71

Baird, John, 49, 51, 67, 77–78, 83; death of, 152; at Eski Zagra, 48; studying Albanian language, 74; work with

Albanians in Monastir, 73; writes Gerasim Kyrias's obituary, 177

Balkans, descriptions of, 159–161

Bansko, church organized at, 46–47; religious movement at, 44; summer training class at, 95

Bebek Seminary, 26; Albanian applicants to, 27

Bibles (Bible portions), Albanian translation of, 88; Bulgarian translation of, 86–87; distribution of, 8, 11, 13, 40, 52, 63, 81, 113

Bible Lands Missions' Aid Society, funding Monastir orphanage, 107

Bible Women, 72, 81, 95

Bitola. See Monastir

Bond, Fannie, medical work of in Monastir, 68–69; retirement after thirty-six years, 102; tours, 90, 93

Bond, Lewis, 69, 84, 103; pastor in church at Monastir, 80; preaching in Kortcha, 88; retirement after thirty-six years, 102; tours, 90, 93

books and pamphlets, 2, 4, 6, 11–12, 15, 35, 38, 45, 50, 57, 65, 81, 113, 122–123

Bowman, Cecile B., appointed to Albania for educational work, 143–144

British and Foreign Bible Society (BFBS), 123; centennial of, 105; translation of the New Testament, xi; work in Albania, 74

Bulgaria and Bulgarians, 25, 33, 82, 160; beginning of ABCFM work at, 86; descriptions of, 27; diplomatic ties with the United States, 154; education, 34, 36; evangelism of, 83; Methodists in, 86; nationalism and struggle for independence, 34, 38, 43; a reading people, 25; religion, 13, 34, 36; thirst for the Word of God, 25, 28, 41

Bulgarian Evangelical Society, 67, 115

Canning, Sir Stratford, 15

Cilka. See Tsilka

Clarke, Elizabeth, in Sofia, 98

Clarke, William, 153; acting pastor at Monastir church, 107; report from, 111; work in Kortcha, 112

Cole, Harriet, 69, 71, 79, 83, 89, 108; illness and retirement, 115

colportage and colporteurs, 29, 68, 81, 89, 105, 113, 117

Constantinople, 82, 166; Albanians at Gedik Pasha school, 167; Bible distribution from, 45; Gedik Pasha school at, 139; printing press at, 87

Index

Crawford, Sophia, arrival in Monastir, 62

Dako, Christo, Christian missionary in Kortcha, 131; graduate of Oberlin College, School of Theology, 145

Dako, Sevasti Kyrias. *See* Qiriazi, Sevasti

Durazzo (Durres), 135

Dwight, 9; tour in Macedonia, 10-11

Elbasan, boys' boarding school at, 147, 155, 157; desire for schools, 131; mission property in, 130; Phineas and Violet Kennedy at, 133–134; private worship meetings at, 130–131; public worship meetings forbidden, 130; suitable mission station, 115

Epirus, 14

Erickson, Charles and Carrie, xiv, 130, 132, 142, 144, 148, 150; arrested, 135; calls for the evangelization of Albania, 131; exile from Tirana, 115, 130; sent to Kortcha, 111; visit to USA to advocate for the Albanians, 133, 140–142; work in Italy with Albanians, 148, 151–152, 154; work in Tirana, 115

Eski Zagra, 34, 48, 50; girls boarding school 40, 44–45

European Turkey, 33; Moslems friendly, 39; population statistics, 31

French military, 153

Greece and Greeks, 12-15; antipathy to strangers, 14; religion of, 14; schools, 12, 15

gypsies, 60, 69

Hamlin, Cyrus, xii, 13; tours in Bulgaria, 86

Haskell, Edward, 115, 152; opens school in Kortcha, 112–113; refugee work at, 136; transferred to Salonica, 80; working in Monastir, 78, 113

Hawley, Hilda, appointed to Albania for medical work, 143; in Salonica, 148

Hay, John (U.S. Secretary of State), 96

Haystack Prayer Meeting, vii-viii

Holway, Theodore and Elizabeth, in Monastir, 102

House, John, 102; at Eski Zagra, 48; report from, 99; at Salonica, 80, 102, 123

Ionian Islands, 4

Ioannina. *See* Joannini

illiteracy, xi–xii

Illyriac, 5

insurrections, hostilities, political agitation, unrest and war, 53–54, 62, 69, 71, 82–83,

94, 99–103, 113, 123, 127–128, 134–136, 142, 144, 153

Istanbul. *See* Constantinople

Izmir. *See* Smyrna

Jenney, Edward and Kate, 49, 51, 55–56; letters from, 53, 65

Jews, x, 16, 24–25, 31, 34, 89, 126, 146, 150; in Albania, 23

Joannini (Ioannina), 12

Kennedy, Phineas and Violet, xiv, 116, 130, 144, 148, 150, 152, 160; expelled to Salonica, 136, 147; preaching work, 160; relief work, 138; sent to Kortcha, 110–112; temporarily in Elbasan, 133–134; withdraw from ABCFM, 164; work with women, 151

King, Jonas, 9, 11-12

Kortcha (Korça), boys' school started at, 112–113, 116; center of the Albanian work, 105; church services at, 88, 109, 116, 131, 160; Ladies' Literary Society at, 139; made a full ABCFM station, 112; night school at, 116, 139; Sunday School at, 109, 111, 160; taken by Greeks, 135; work with Wallachians at, 88

Kortcha (Korça) Girls' School, 80–81, 88, 93, 98, 101, 109, 116, 119, 123, 126, 131, 139, 146–147; attempts by government to close, 130; Bible study at, 91; Board of Trustees for, 145, 147, 155; boarding students received, 93; called "the Kyrias School", 145; Christian Endeavor Society at, 160; closed in wartime conditions, 155; an evangelical school, 123; Greek seizure of, 138; Muslim girls compelled to withdraw from, 88; only Albanian school for girls, 88, 101; opposed by Greek bishop, 105; problems with the government about the use of Albanian, 107, 110, 112; property of, 107; religious services at, 108; supported by Women's Board of Missions, 157; Thanas Sina teacher at, 91

Kurds and Kurdish, 124–125, 129, 158

Kyrias, Gerasim (Gjerasim Qiriazi), 77; death of, 78–79; ordained, xiv, 74; founder of Evangelical Brotherhood, xiv; obituary, 177; work in Uskup (Skopje), 65

Kyrias, Gjergj (Gjergj Qiriazi), hymnbooks of, 47

Kyrias, Paraskevi (Parashqevi Qiriazi), directing the Kortcha Girls' School, 108

Kyrias, Sevasti (Sevasti Qiriazi), 91; forced to leave Kortcha by Greek occupation, 147; heroic journey to Kortcha, 105; respected by ABCFM missionaries, 93

Locke, William and Zoe, in Monastir, 67

London Missionary Society, 8

Long, A. L., 30, 38, 86

Lowndes, Isaac, 8

Macedonia, descriptions of, 128–129

Malta, 8; printing press x, 4

Maltbie, Esther, 110

Marsh, George, 49, 51; at Eski Zagra, 48; letter from, 49

Matthews, Mary, 89, 153, 161; life in peril in Monastir, 153–154; report from, 85–86; studying Albanian, 85; work in Monastir, 83, 151, 157

medical work, in Albania, 125, 131–132, 143; offering of 10,000 USD for an Albanian hospital, 133, 140

Methodists (American Methodist Episcopal Society), 30, 40, 109–110; asked by ABCFM to work in Albania, 165–166; working in Bulgaria, 86; working in Serbia, 163

Mills, Samuel, vii, ix

missionaries, arrested by Greeks in Salonica, 158; avoiding politics, x, 59, 100, 159; helped by British and French surgeons, 156; learning languages, x; relief efforts of, 53–54, 100, 105, 152; seeking to promote love and tolerance in the Levant, 159; touring work, 76, 83, 94, 100, 113; wives, 41, 52, 76, 83

Mitrovitza, 94

Moldavia, 9, 11

Monastir (Bitola), 28-29, 83, 87–89; Albanian language spoken at, 51; boys boarding school at, 88; church at, 55–56, 58, 60, 63, 66-69, 72, 80, 92, 107, 111–112, 114; fire at, 154; mission station at, 49, 51, 80, 84, 92–93, 101; religious discussions at, 52; Sunday School, 101; taken by Serbians, 135, 138; tours to regions around, 64–65

Monastir Girls' School, 58, 61, 63, 66, 69–71, 75–76, 79, 81–83, 85–86, 89, 93, 99, 106, 108–109, 112, 115, 120, 123, 126, 137–138, 146, 156–157; Albanian students at, 85, 91; boarding students, 101; Bulgarian teachers, 85; Christian Endeavor Society at, 85–86, 88, 106; closure of, 156; an evangelical school, 109, 120; lectures to be given in English, 85, 89, 157; orphan care, 103, 106–107, 156; religious nature of, 85, 92; Young People's Society of Christian Endeavor at, 85–86, 106

Monospetovo, 69

Morea, 4, 8

Murtino, conference of Protestant churches at, 89

Orthodox Church and bishops, 61, 65, 68; opposition to Kortcha Girls' School, 105; opposition to liturgy in mother tongue, 88

Parsons, tour to Bulgaria and Macedonia, 23

pastors and preachers, 72, 83; native (indigenous) preachers and workers, 41, 62, 76, 88, 111, 113; need for, 73, 79, 84, 94

Perdicari, Gregory, 5

persecution and religious freedom, 15–16, 30, 37, 68, 98; imprisonment of Protestant converts, 37; seizure of printing presses, 37

Philippopolis (Plovdiv), 64, 118; boys school 40-41; 43

politics, x, 59, 100, 158

Presbyterian Board of Missions, asked by ABCFM to work in Albania, 165

Prilep (Perlepe), 58, 61

Prishtina, Serbian school at, 94

Protestantism, official recognition in the Ottoman Empire, 17-18, 20-23; respected in Macedonia, 71; seeking recognition in Monastir, 90–91

Qiriazi (Gjerasim, Sevasti, Gjergj, Parashqevi). *See under* Kyrias

Raiqeva, Marika, 56

Resen, 58

Riggs, Charles, appointed to Albania for agricultural work, 143–144

Riggs, Elias, Bible translation, 87; hymns, 47; literary work, 45; preaching in Bulgarian at Constantinople, 45; tours in Bulgaria, 86

Robert College, xii; forty Bulgarian students at, 46

Roosevelt, President Theodore, 96

Salonica, 9, 81, 95, 101, 113, 166; Agricultural and Industrial Institute at, 104, 123, 152; Albanians at, 102; fire at, 154; Greek Protestant Church at, 115; new station at, 80; Ottoman bank blown up at, 99; refugee work at, 136; Sultan Abdul Hamid I retirement home at, 120; taken by Greeks, 135

Samokov, 43–44, 66, 84, 118; girls' boarding school at, 45, 47–48, 50, 75–76, 84, 122; printing press at, 122–123; theological institute at, *See* American Collegiate and Theological Institute (Samokov)

Schauffler, 9; tour in Macedonia, 10-11

schools, 8, 29, 34

Scutari (Shkodra), 135

Serbia (Servia) and Serbians, 9–10, 23, 27–28, 89, 91–92, 94, 127, 134–135, 137–138, 143, 146, 158, 160–164

Shkodra. *See* Scutari

Shumla, 30

Sinas (Sina), Thanas, arrested, 93–94; pastor of Kortcha church, 88; translation of the Bible, 88, 91

Skopje. *See* Uscup

Smyrna (Izmir), 1, Albanians studying at ABCFM college at, 126, 150

Sofia, 67–68; kindergarten at, 118, 123; Protestant church at, 68, 98

Stafford, LeRoy H., appointed to Albania, 141–142, 144

Stone, Ellen, 133; evangelistic work, 89–90; hostage crisis, 95–99; touring, 90

Strangford, Lady Emily, 54

Strumnitsa, 65, 69

Thessaloniki. *See* Salonica

Tsilka (Cilka), Grigor, 101; in America, 105; arrested for not closing Kortcha school, 112; arrested with Charles Erickson, 135; books and manuscripts seized by authorities, 112; death of (influenza), 156; devoted worker, 156; main worker at Kortcha, 98, 131; preaching in Kortcha, 109, 111; teaching English to boys, 111

Tsilka, Katerina, hostage crisis, 95–99

Turkey and Turks, 11, 14–17, 19, 24–25, 29, 30–32, 34, 38, 46, 77, 82, 87, 95, 97–98, 100, 103, 106, 117, 120–121, 127, 129–130, 134–135, 139, 141, 149–150, 158–159, 167

Uskub (Skopje), 28-29; desire for teachers at, 65; persecution at, 65

Varna, 30

Veqilharxhi, Naum, xii

Wallachia and Wallachians, 9, 11, 27, 69, 88–89

Wied, Prince Wilhelm, 143

women, 41–42, 52, 56, 61, 79, 89–90, 117, 139, 153

Women's Board of Missions, supported Kortcha Girls' School, 157

Yatasha, preaching at, 57–58

Zornitza (Morning Star) (Bulgarian periodical), 38, 50, 87, 108–109, 122–123

Facsimile of Rev. John Baird's obituary for Gerasim Kyrias, from the ABCFM's *Missionary Herald*, May, 1894, 199–200:

THE FIRST PROTESTANT ALBANIAN PREACHER.

BY REV. J. W. BAIRD, OF MONASTIR.

Rev. GERASIM D. KYRIAS, the first Protestant Albanian preacher, was born in Turnovo, near Monastir, in 1858; but with his parents soon removed to Monastir, and attended the Greek school of that place till old enough to learn a trade, when he was apprenticed to a shoemaker. When American missionaries went to that city, in 1873, he sometimes attended services partly out of curiosity and partly out of a love for mischief. Becoming interested he soon accepted and followed the truth, though he met considerable opposition. Soon he began to feel that the Lord had called him to be a preacher, and as he gave good proof of deep piety and good ability he was received into the mission school at Samokov, where, in 1882, he finished the course, leaving an excellent reputation for scholarship, ability, faithfulness, energy, geniality, and piety.

While preaching in Bulgarian, in Uskub, he received a call to the superintendency of the colporters of the British and Foreign Bible Society in Macedonia and Albania. Seeing here an opening for work among his

REV. G. D. KYRIAS.

countrymen, spiritually neglected for centuries, he entered upon and devoted himself to the evangelization of the Albanians, translating, putting books through the press, writing hymns, and preaching the gospel. While on one of his tours, in November, 1884, he was seized by brigands and held for six months, suffering intense and prolonged hardship. It was a wonder that even his strong constitution endured such a strain. When released he resumed his work with new zeal, not only preaching but especially conversing with men about spiritual things and pressing upon them the claims of God. For this latter work he had a special talent. He planned a school for girls, and after his ordination as an evangelist, in 1890, removed permanently to Kortcha, and with the assistance of his sister began the school, which, in spite of fierce opposition from the Greek ecclesiastics, grew rapidly. He was successful in getting funds to buy a place for a school and chapel. This is probably the only Albanian girls' school that has been opened. The Greek Church, to which all the southern Albanians who have not become Moslems belong, has uniformly refrained from supporting Abanian schools, from encouraging any religious book, and from the use of the Albanian language in the churches, so that to this day she has not given them a page in their mother-tongue and now would gladly prevent anyone from using the Albanian language. As the printing of tracts was not possible, Mr. Kyrias wrote many letters to acquaintances on religious subjects. Worn out with labor he took a hard cold, and though he sought relief in Monastir, died in that city of consumption, January 2, 1894. His last days were peaceful.

Mr. Kyrias was a born leader, a tireless worker, an attractive and impressive preacher, and a spiritually minded man. Where is the man or men who will take up the work from which the Lord has called this pioneer evangelist?

INSTITUTE *for* ALBANIAN & PROTESTANT STUDIES

The mission of the Institute for Albanian and Protestant Studies is to promote the discovery of Albanian and Protestant history and thought.

This book is part of the 500/200 Series published in commemoration of the 500th anniversary of the Protestant Reformation in Europe, the 200th anniversary of the Albanian Bible translation project, the 150th anniversary of the publication of the Gheg Albanian Gospels, and the 125th anniversaries of the Albanian Evangelical Brotherhood and the Albanian Girls' School in Kortcha. Other titles in this series include:

- *Albania and the Albanians in the Annual Reports of the British and Foreign Bible Society, 1805–1955*
- *My Life: the autobiography of the pioneer of female education in Albania, Sevasti Kyrias Dako*
- *Gerasim Kyrias and the Albanian National Awakening, 1858–1894* (John Quanrud)
- *Captured by Brigands* (Gerasim Kyrias)
- *Travels in Albania, Selected Writings from British Authoresses, 1717–1878*

www.instituti.org

Colophon

Front cover:
"Bridge over the Drachor, Monastir" by Mary Adelaide Walker in *Through Macedonia to the Albanian Lakes* (London: Chapman and Hall, 1864), page 157.

Back cover:
Workers of the Kortcha Girls' School and Protestant mission station, ca. 1911. *Standing, left to right*: Fanka Eftimova, Paraskevi Kyrias, Marianthi Petro, Efigjeni Janaqis. *Seated, left to right*: Phineas and Violet Bond Kennedy, Sevasti Kyrias Dako, and Christo Dako.

Dedication:
This work is dedicated by the editor to Arben Bushgjokaj, Albanian pastor, educator, expert in American literature, and – with his wife Linda – dear friends of many years.

www.ingramcontent.com/pod-product-compliance
Lightning Source LLC
Chambersburg PA
CBHW031443040426
42444CB00007B/941